W9-ABW-254

TAIL GUNNER

TAIL GUNNER

SQUADRON LEADER R.C. RIVAZ DFC

Foreword by Group Captain Leonard Cheshire
VC, DSO, DFC

SUTTON PUBLISHING

First published in 1943 by Jarrolds

First published in this new edition 1996 by
Sutton Publishing Limited · Phoenix Mill
Thrupp · Stroud · Gloucestershire · GL5 2BU

British Library Cataloguing in Publication Data
A catalogue card for this book is available from the British Library

ISBN 0 7509 1327 4

 ALAN SUTTON™ and SUTTON™ are the
trade marks of Sutton Publishing Limited

Printed in Great Britain by
Hartnolls Limited
Bodmin, Cornwall.

FOREWORD

BY GROUP CAPTAIN LEONARD CHESHIRE, V.C., D.S.O., D.F.C.

I am very pleased to be associated with the reissue of this book. Flt.-Lt. Rivaz—or 'Revs' as we used to call him—was my first permanent rear gunner, and a close personal friend. He was, without doubt, one of the best gunners with whom I ever flew, and for something like two years we shared the difficulties of war. He, through no fault of his, lost his life; I, through the Grace of God, was spared mine.

Revs was older than the average air crew, and he took the war more seriously than many of us, to whom it was alternatively a wonderful adventure and a confounded nuisance. He never mixed very freely in the Mess, yet he seemed to be happy when others were enjoying themselves, and he was popular and respected—which under the circumstances was unusual and therefore a tribute to his character. While we would run off on leave to the bright lights (if such they can be called in war), he would go on a farm to help with the work; cleaning out stables and so on. This to him was the perfect holiday.

The dinghy episode, which you will read in this book, typifies Revs' cool and calm, bringing with him a little common sense when things got out of hand; not the dashing leader, but the backbone, complementing and blending with the others. When I, as the captain of the crew, was away, he would keep a fatherly eye on the others; and I think that most of us went to him with our troubles. On the evening that Taffy, once our navigator, went out on what was to prove his last trip, Revs accompanied him to his aircraft and lingered longer than usual. His wave was Taffy's farewell.

Tail Gunner, Revs' autobiography, was written in the

midst of war, and is told with great sincerity. It gives a true and fine picture of the dangers and discomforts of a tail gunner's life, and I am sure that there are many for whom it will bring back forgotten memories. For me personally it brings back the memory of the many fallen, but for whom we ourselves would not be enjoying peace today. I wish it every success.

Leonard Cheshire.

INTRODUCTION

Squadron Leader Dick Rivaz – A Biographical Note

Richard Rivaz was born in Assam, India, on 15 March 1908, the son of a colonial official in the Indian Civil Service. Dick returned to England with his parents while still a child and later studied painting at the Royal College of Art. During the 1930s he became an accomplished artist with a studio in Chelsea and exhibited at the Royal Academy of Arts in Piccadilly. Unable to make a good living from painting he decided to train as a teacher and took up an appointment at Collyer's School in Horsham, Sussex, where he taught art and physical training.

Volunteering for pilot training with the RAF in 1940, Dick was bitterly disappointed when he learned that, at thirty-two, he was too old to become a pilot. He finally commenced his training as an air-gunner in May and first saw operational service in Bomber Command flying the twin-engined Whitley Mk V with No. 102 Squadron from Topcliffe, Yorkshire, in August 1940, where he crewed up as rear gunner to Leonard Cheshire. Dick later transferred to No. 35 Squadron in March 1941 to complete his tour as an air-gunner, again in Leonard Cheshire's crew, but this time flying the Halifax Mk II from Linton-on-Ouse. During this tour he took part in many night bombing attacks against heavily defended enemy targets like Duisberg, Düsseldorf and Essen. In July 1941 he was involved in a dramatic shoot-out with German fighters over La Rochelle in broad daylight for which he was awarded the DFC.

On two night raids to Cologne with No. 102 Squadron, the first in late 1940 and the second in early 1941, he narrowly escaped death. The first occasion was on the night of 12/13 November when his Whitley was set on fire by an exploding flare inside the fuselage. For his skill in flying the crippled bomber back to its home base the captain, Pilot Officer Leonard Cheshire, was awarded the DSO. His badly injured wireless operator, Sergeant Davidson, received the DFM.

The second time was returning from Cologne on 1 March 1941 when Whitley V, T4261, S for Sugar, captained by

Squadron Leader C.E. Florigny, ditched in the sea off the Norfolk coast shortly before midnight. Florigny was last seen standing on top of the fuselage but was unable to reach the dinghy which was being blown away from the aircraft by the strong wind. Dick and the three other surviving crew members spent eight hours in the dinghy before being rescued.

Subsequently Dick was rescued a second time from the Channel while flying with No. 35 Squadron. His Halifax Mk II, V9978, A for Apple, captained by the squadron CO, Wing Commander Basil Robinson DFC, was forced to ditch some 60 miles off the English coast returning from a daylight raid on Brest. With this raid, Dick completed his tour of operations.

He instructed at the Central Gunnery School from January to August 1942 before being posted to Canada to train as a pilot. When Dick finally returned to England he was destined not to fly again operationally, but instead toured the country with the Ministry of Aircraft Production and ferried aircraft with the Air Transport Auxiliary. At the end of the war Dick was collecting material for a history of RAF Transport Command when, on 13 October 1945, the Liberator transport aircraft in which he was a passenger caught fire on take-off from Brussels airport, killing all on board. Dick Rivaz was thirty-seven years old.

JF August 1996

CHAPTER I

I WILL start by introducing Leonard Cheshire. I introduce him at the beginning as he was my first operational pilot, the first pilot who flew me over Germany. I will leave the details of my training and begin when I went to my first squadron straight from the Operational Training Unit.

I arrived at 102 Squadron, Topcliffe, one evening in August 1940, feeling very new and shy, and rather wondering what sort of people I should meet and how they would treat a new boy like myself. The only operational crews I had seen was when an odd crew had landed at Abingdon on their way home after a raid. These people had always been dressed in flying boots and were wearing no collars or ties, but had silk scarves knotted round their necks, and they were usually unshaven and with unbrushed hair. I had looked on them as some sort of gods and wondered whether one day I, too, should be privileged to walk about and look as they did. These were the people I should be meeting now and with whom I should have to live. Somehow they did not seem to me to be ordinary normal people, but people either with charmed lives or else lives that would soon not be theirs . . . and I thought this would surely be visible in either their appearance or behaviour.

I was quite surprised to find that the Officers' Mess was very similar to the one I had just left. I arrived after supper, and found my way to the ante-room, where the wireless was on, apparently unnoticed by anyone in the room. There were some people lolling in deep black leather arm-chairs, reading; one or two were asleep. There was a group standing round the empty fireplace with pint beer-tankards in their hands. Some were writing letters, and four were playing cards at a table in the middle of the room. Everyone there looked perfectly normal; in fact, the whole scene, as I surveyed it, was just the same as could be seen in the ante-room of the Mess I had just left, or, indeed, in any other Mess. One or two people I noticed were wearing the ribbon of the D.F.C. These people I stared at, probably too long, as one stares at celebrities or personalities

9

of importance, hoping to read the signs of some of their experiences written in their faces. But they, too, looked perfectly ordinary and completely unconscious and oblivious of their distinction. Those talking to them did not seem to be treating them with any particular respect or showing them any deference, but were conversing with them as they might with any ordinary being.

I wandered out of the Mess feeling that perhaps life would not be so different, after all.

I went in search of the duty batman, and was told that the Mess was very full at the moment and that I would have to share a room. I was taken to my room—or, rather, part share of the room—and found the other occupant already in bed and asleep. This other occupant, whom I was later to know as Leonard, was lying absolutely still and silent and fast asleep. I have very rarely known Leonard to go to bed at the average person's time, but either very early or excessively late. At whichever time he went he would sleep until he was awakened, and then get up perfectly fresh.

He had scattered his clothes all over the place: some were on my bed, some were on his bed, and some were on the floor. Also on my bed there was an open suit-case, two tennis racquets, a squash racquet, and his towel. I removed the articles from my bed to the floor, making as little noise as I could, although I need not have been so cautious as nothing other than a vigorous shaking will awaken Leonard once he is asleep. I looked at his tunic, thrown carelessly over the back of a chair, to see if I could gain some clue as to the identity of this unknown person. I saw he was a pilot-officer, like myself; also that he was a pilot. I also noticed that he had no *gong* up, and thought therefore that he, too, might be a new-comer. I could not see much of the sleeper, as only the top of his head, showing brown untidy hair, was visible above the bedclothes.

I went to bed wondering what my new companion and this new life would be like.

.   .   .   .   .

I was awakened next morning by the buzzing sound of an electric razor, and saw a slight figure in brightly coloured pyjamas walking up and down the room trailing a length of electric flex behind him and running the razor in a care-free manner up and down his face. After a few moments I said "Good morning" . . . and was favoured with some sort of grunt in reply. Undismayed, I started asking questions about the new station and my new squadron, but to all my questions the only replies I got were grunts. Eventually I gave up my questioning as a bad job and started to get up.

I saw this uncommunicative and, as I thought, strange person several times during the day, but never once did he show that he recognized me. I noticed that he seemed to know everybody, and that most people called him *Cheese*.

That night I changed my room.

CHAPTER II

AFTER breakfast on that first day I went up to see the C.O., a charming man who made me feel quite at home and very happy. He told me I was in 'B' Flight, and sent me down to see my Flight Commander, whom I later learnt was familiarly known as 'Teddy'. He was an excitable little man with an enormous backside and proportionately large moustache.

As I stood at the door of his office he was on the telephone, and I heard him say, "But I don't want any more gunners: I've got all the gunners I want." As he hung up the receiver he called me in and said, "That was you I was talking about."

'Not so good,' I thought.

He told me to shut the door. I found him much more pleasant than I first thought. He explained that I should not be put on a crew yet as there were no vacancies, and that it was up to me to learn all I could in the meantime.

He sent me to see the squadron gunnery leader, who was the oldest and toughest gunner I had as yet seen, and who was known as 'Steve'. He was about forty-five and looked as hard as nails, but had two of the kindest eyes imaginable. He was sometimes known as 'Two-gun Steve', as he used to carry a couple of revolvers and a jack-knife . . . which made his tunic stick out from his waist as though it had been starched.

Everyone seemed to like and respect him. He had been an observer in the last war; later became a pilot, and was now an air-gunner. He had an amazing capacity for work, and seemed to expect other people to have the same. He had one of the deepest and loudest voices I have ever heard, and was never afraid of using it. He always said exactly what he thought of people and in no uncertain language—his vocabulary for swear words being terrific.

He took me straight out to an aeroplane to see what I knew, or, rather, what I did not know—as he did not seem in the least interested in the little I did know. He spent the rest of the morning teaching me and showing me around.

I soon got really fond of Steve. If he thought anyone was keen to learn, he would do anything he could to help that person, but, on the other hand, if he thought people were slacking, he would have no further use for them at all.

He used to smoke the foulest-smelling cigarettes, which he rolled himself and used to say in defence of numerous protests that when he smoked he wanted something he could taste. He also had one of the largest appetites I have ever seen in anybody. He taught me a tremendous amount about gunnery during my early days with the squadron, and used to maintain that everybody should know as much as possible about the aeroplane in which they would have to fly, quite apart from their own particular job.

I was not to know Steve for long, as he was killed on an operational trip a few months after I joined the squadron.

.   .   .   .   .

About a week after my arrival I was sitting in the ante-room after lunch writing a letter thanking a friend for 'Ming'. Ming had arrived that morning by post, and was my mascot; he was a tiny stuffed baby panda, and I had him in my pocket while I was writing. The air-raid siren sounded, and I looked out of the window and saw people running to the shelters.

'Good lord!' I thought, 'what on earth is all the rush about? . . .'

The ante-room, which had been crowded a few seconds before, was almost empty, and the few remaining were rushing to the door.

'Extraordinary!' I thought.

While the siren was still going there came an unearthly screaming noise. All other sounds were then promptly drowned by the loudest explosion I had ever heard, and the windows of the ante-room were blown in with a din like several rifle-shots. I left my letter and ran to the door.

'This is something like,' I thought. 'This is action—real fun and excitement. . . .'

I had never heard a bomb burst at close quarters before, and I thought how splendid it was to be seeing some real action. I saw someone crouching behind a sofa in the hall as more bombs burst outside and the whole building shook.

The next thing I remember was lying on my face in a passage, covered with dust and choking and surrounded by broken glass and rubble. I got to my feet and saw through a cloud of smoke that the Mess a few feet behind me was a complete ruin: bricks and plaster, dust and glass, were piled up together. 'This is frightful,' I thought, and once more found myself on my face with the roof trembling and shaking as another stick of bombs fell across the Mess—one bursting a few feet in front of me and completely blocking the passage.

I lay on the floor gasping for breath; choking and panting while bombs burst all around. I could hear the whine of diving aeroplanes and the scream of falling bombs while all the time the ground shook with the explosions. I was really frightened, more frightened than I had ever been before. I noticed that there was someone else lying on the floor beside me, and we clung to each other.

"This is *bloody*, isn't it?" I said.

Outside there was a new noise added to the din: it was a sort of loud crackling sound and was a building burning just outside. The air was filled with fumes and smoke and dust which were almost suffocating; my lungs felt as if they were dry and empty, and I gasped and choked.

The inferno seemed to have moved a bit farther off, so my companion and I got to our feet and climbed over bricks and stones and rubble, and made our way outside. Dust and smoke were everywhere, and it was impossible to see more than a few feet. We ran to the nearest shelter and went inside.

The first person I saw was the C.O., who said to me, "This is a funny sort of welcome for you!" My tunic was grey with dust and badly torn, and blood was trickling down my face. "You'd better go and see the M.O. when it quietens down," the C.O. said.

I remembered Ming in my pocket, and decided that that should be his home from then on. He has accompanied me on all my operational trips, and still resides there as I write.

When all was quiet I joined the group surveying what remained of our Mess. I noticed that not only had bombs burst within a few yards and on two sides of me, but that one had also burst slap overhead. The roof and wall of the room above where I had been lying had disappeared, and I saw a bed standing by itself and clothes strewn all over the debris. Steve joined us, covered from head to foot in dust. He had been lying in a ditch not far from the Mess, watching the fray through a pair of binoculars. He said he had a grand view until he was buried by earth and plaster, which completely obstructed his vision. This infuriated him, particularly as by the time he had extricated himself the show was over!

I went up to the hangars to see what damage had been done there. They had been badly knocked about, and one was on fire: the fire party were at work with their hoses amid a great din of crackling and sizzling.

In another hangar a Wing Commander was at work with a gang of men, all in tin hats, clearing debris from the floor. I went to join them and was promptly bellowed at by the Wing Commander.

"What the hell do you think you're doing? . . . Why haven't you got a tin hat? . . . Can't you see the roof is falling in? . . . Do you want to get brained? . . . If you *want* something to do, go and help move that Whitley; there's an unexploded bomb beside it! . . . When you've done that, go and wash all that blood off your face, and get it seen to!"

I thought that working beside an unexploded bomb that might go off at any moment was far more dangerous than working in the hangar, but I did not say so, and went and helped push the Whitley away.

On my way to Sick Quarters I saw a party of men digging furiously around a shelter that had received a direct hit: the ambulance was there, and the orderlies were lifting a man—with his tunic, face, and hair covered with earth—on to a stretcher. Someone put a cigarette between his lips and lit it for him. Sweat was pouring off his face and caking the earth . . . and I noticed that his legs were in an unnatural twisted position. Someone was digging around another pair of legs: the body was still buried and the legs obviously broken. I saw two more men crushed—with faces nearly the same colour as their tunics—between sheets of corrugated iron: they were both dead.

I decided that my own minor cuts could wait, and went to my room, and found the windows blown in and a chunk of bomb splinter through my bed!

That night the siren went again just as I was dropping off to sleep. I was in the shelter about a hundred yards away before the siren had finished wailing! I was not the first one there, either!

.   .   .   .   .

I had returned from leave some time later, and the first person I saw when I got inside the Mess was Leonard. "I've got you in my crew," he said.

"Grand," I replied. "Thanks awfully."

"Don't thank me. You've not flown with me yet," he said . . . and smiled. Leonard's smile is really beautiful: his mouth, instead of getting bigger, seems to get smaller, and his eyes shine. When he smiles he makes you feel glad: it is a smile meant for you, and you alone.

"We'll have a talk tomorrow," he continued, "and I'll tell you all the things I want you to do. We might be on ops tomorrow night."

I think this was about the first time Leonard had spoken to me; certainly he had never said as much before. I was really happy. I was in a crew at last, and I wanted to tell everyone I saw: I wanted to sing and jump about, to talk to everybody. I felt friendly towards them all.

I was not pleased about being in Leonard's crew particularly, anybody's crew would have done; in fact, if I had had the chance, I would probably have chosen anyone but Leonard. But I did not know Leonard then. I don't suppose for a moment that he had chosen me, either: it was just one of those things that happen.

I was going to fly operationally! That was what I kept telling myself, and what my heart had been set on ever since I had started to fly. I wanted to fly on operations . . . to see bombs burst and see fires! . . . to see flak and shoot down fighters! . . . and now I was going to start, maybe tomorrow night! My leave was forgotten . . . *and* the rather depressed feeling I had had when I entered the Mess: *everything* was forgotten except that I was going to fly over Germany!

When Leonard said "I've got you in my crew" I became so excited that I stayed awake a long time that night thinking about my new fortune, and wondering where I should be at the same time the following night.

CHAPTER III

I SAT next to Leonard the following morning at breakfast, and found him already midway through a huge bowl of porridge. He always seems to have a big appetite, and has an amazing way with waiters, and usually, in consequence, gets far more to eat than other people. I have often heard him say in his quiet, serious voice to one of the Mess waiters, *"I don't think I can manage three eggs this morning, two will be enough!"* . . . and he will be brought two while the rest of us are given one! He has his stock phrases of humour which he never tires of using; I have heard them dozens of times, and I hope I will hear them dozens more times! Most people never know if he is being serious or not: he speaks in such a serious voice and with such a serious expression on his face. One of his pet remarks is—when he is about to sit down next to someone already seated—"Don't get up!"—at the same time raising his hand as though that person is about to rise. Another time, when you are reading a letter, he will lean across and say to you—"After you with that when you've finished." It rather non-plusses him if you pass the letter across to him! Or again, if he hears someone say "Good God!"—he will say: "Yes . . . what is it?" The person will probably say—or so Leonard hopes—"I only said 'Good God'." Leonard will then reply: "Oh! I thought you were addressing me." All these expressions have been tried on me many times, and I have now got the right answers!

"We are *on* tonight," Leonard said, turning to me.

"Splendid! D'you know where?"

"Yes, but keep it quiet! . . . *Italy!*"

Oh, boy! what a magnificent trip to start off with!

Leonard had plenty of work for me to do that day: he wanted to know how much I knew about the aeroplane. How much morse did I know? Could I find everything in my turret in the dark? Did I know how to launch the flares? What did I know about dinghy drill? Did I know how to bale out? Could I map-read? Could I operate the emergency hand-pump for the under-carriage? Did I know where the petrol cocks were? and so on. . . .

He introduced me to the rest of his crew. There was
Desmond, our second pilot, a large fair-haired man of about
twenty-two. He was magnificently built and seemed to be in a
permanent daydream, and I thought he looked more like a
poet than a pilot; I had often seen him before, exercising a
bloodhound around the aerodrome. Then there was Taffy, our
navigator, all smiles and friendly at once. The other member
was Stokie, our wireless operator, and, as Leonard said, one of
the best wireless operators in the Air Force and afraid of
nothing. Leonard was very proud of his crew, and I hoped
that one day I should come up to the standard of the
others.

We did our Night Flying Test that morning, and Leonard
kept calling me up on the intercom. I was beginning to feel
that I was very fortunate in my new pilot. After we landed he
wanted to know what I thought of the turret, and if everything
was all right.

All that day I kept saying to myself, 'We're going to Italy
tonight!' I could not have been more excited if I had been
going there on a holiday, or if I had been going to some
marvellous party. Life, I felt, was just beginning: I was a
member of an operational crew, and would soon be doing my
first operations! This was what I had been waiting for, and
for what I had been longing!

It started to rain that afternoon, and was still drizzling as
we dressed in our flying clothing: Leonard asked me if I had
on plenty of clothes, as I would probably be cold. We drove
out to our aeroplane in the drizzling rain and had to wade the
last hundred yards or so through mud. The ground crew were
waiting for us, sheltering under the wings.

We quickly got inside out of the rain, and I went straight
to my turret. Almost as soon as I had settled myself a message
was brought saying that the operation had been *scrubbed*
I will not attempt to describe my disappointment . . . nor the
anger of the others.

.   .   .   .   .

The following night we were briefed to go to Dortmund,
in the Ruhr. I was disappointed it was not to be Italy, but,
as Leonard said, there would be plenty of other opportunities;
anyway, I was delighted at the thought of going anywhere.

All that day I kept looking at the weather and was on tenter-hooks lest we had a repetition of the previous night. However, we did get off all right this time.

It was dark when we took off . . . and, I thought, very mysterious and exciting: I had flown many times at night before, but never on such a marvellous mission. Until we were actually airborne I was worried lest the trip should be cancelled at the last moment. I was interested and thrilled with every word spoken down the intercom.; it was all important and seemed to presage great things to come.

It was a pitch-dark night, and I could not see anything on the ground below me. Leonard and Taffy had quite a lot to say about the navigation: I kept silent, absorbing it all, rather as a child takes in the conversation of its elders.

Occasionally Leonard called me up to ask how I was or if I was cold; after we crossed our coast he told me to test my guns. I had them all ready loaded, and cocked and pressed the trigger. There were yellow flashes from the muzzles of the guns as they fired, and I watched the incendiary bullets—looking like illuminated dots—leaving the guns and retreating rapidly in a curve as they disappeared into the night. There was a smell of burning cordite which I knew quite well and rather liked; it overcame for a few minutes the rather sickly oily smell peculiar to gun turrets. I told Leonard that all the guns were O.K., and he replied "Good show!"

Desmond flew most of the way over the sea, but Leonard took over again as we crossed the Dutch coast. I could just see the coast line below me, and felt a peculiar thrill as I realized we were over enemy occupied territory. Leonard told me to let him know if I saw any lights or anything. Everything from now on would be completely new to me . . . and I was very excited and ready to be entertained!

I saw some searchlights in the distance which looked exactly like our own, except that in amongst their beams there were little flashes of light rather like jewels sparkling, and I thought rather pretty. I told Leonard what I saw, and he said we should probably see some a lot closer later on. I saw several lights on the ground below us, all of which I reported: some were quite bright lights, while others I could hardly see, but they all interested me intensely and I tried to imagine what they were and what was happening below.

When I was not glancing at the ground I was staring out into the night, wondering if I should see any fighters. I kept looking about me up and down to the front and to either side: the moon had risen but was in its last quarter, and I wondered how far I really could see. Until one is thoroughly used to searching the sky at night one's eyes get very dazed and tired, probably because one is trying to take in too much, but with practice it is possible to focus the eyes at a given range and look, as it were, *at* something instead of merely staring out into the distance, when one can be looking yet not really seeing. Try sitting in a dark room and looking out into the night for eight or nine hours, and you will see what I mean.

As we neared the target Leonard and Taffy had further discussions as landmarks they recognized appeared . . . *or landmarks they expected to see did not appear.* I tried to make something out of those light and dark patches on the ground which seemed to mean so much to them.

Taffy said our E.T.A.[1] was up, and we should be over Dortmund. Leonard started to fly round in a wide circle and cursed the darkness. We continued to fly round in a circle for some time, with occasionally Leonard or Taffy making some remark. I thought it seemed very tame and quiet, as I had imagined we should be seeing searchlights and flak, and all sorts of things . . . and I was rather disappointed.

Leonard must have spotted the target, for he said, "There it is, down on the port side. I'm going to fly away and come in right over it! . . . Get ready to drop the bombs, Taffy."

I felt a renewal of excitement, and wondered if I should see the bombs burst: I wanted to very much. I could hear Taffy giving Leonard directions over the intercom. as he watched the target through the bomb sight. At each turn that Taffy gave I could feel the aeroplane instantly change from its course. Taffy was saying "Left . . . left . . . steady! Right! . . . Steady . . . steady . . . *Bombs gone!*"

Almost at the same moment that Taffy said "Bombs gone!" I saw a number of bright flashes on the ground: there seemed to be hundreds of them . . . and almost immediately we were surrounded by flashes and crashes and bangs, and seemed to be the centre of some wild excitement of lights and noise. Leonard must have been doing some violent things with the

[1] Estimated Time of Arrival.

aeroplane, for the ground—now clearly visible by its flashes of light—instead of appearing below us, seemed to be tilting from side to side and at times appeared to be almost overhead. Now and again the aeroplane lurched violently and then dropped, as an explosion louder than the rest was felt and heard below us. So this was what flak was like! I began to wonder if it was much fun, after all . . . in fact, I thought it looked and sounded extremely dangerous.

"I've only dropped one stick," I heard Taffy say.

"O.K.," Leonard replied. "I'll fly in again. Let's see if we can get rid of this stuff first, though."

'They don't seem much concerned,' I thought. 'Perhaps to them this is just an ordinary occurrence . . . something they experience each time they bomb.' I did not know if it was more violent than usual . . . or average . . . or perhaps even rather mild: what I *did* know was that I did not like it! I had heard stories of flak. . . . 'Almost blew us out of the sky!' . . . 'Could feel it hitting us!' . . . or 'Came back full of holes!' . . . but these words meant nothing to me. I had seen aeroplanes come back with holes through them, and rather envied the crews their experiences, but I had no idea what it would really be like, and now I was beginning to find out. There were dozens of search-lights on us, and every dive or climb or turn we did we were still held in their beams. Hundreds of what looked like red and yellow and green balls of fire were hurtling past us and around us: sometimes they were so close I felt I could stretch out my hand and catch them. I began to feel that each one was aimed at me, and would burst through my turret, but as each one seemed on the point of hitting me it somehow miraculously skimmed past just clear of the tail.

An aeroplane from the ground always looks so small, but when you are flying in one and being shot at, it always seems so large. I was fascinated by this cascade of destructive little lights coming up at us so relentlessly all the time: they seemed to start their journey upward so slowly, but as they came near they whizzed by with incredible speed. I could see the flashes from where those guns started, and fired my guns at them as well as at the searchlights. I fired hundreds of rounds and, for a few minutes, went mad . . . shouting and cursing and laughing all at once. *What was I there for? . . . Why should I not shoot, too? . . . Why should I sit still and be shot at when I had some guns in front of me?* . . . I hoped I was hurting them . . . killing them . . . making them run!

While all these hundreds of coloured balls of fire were popping up at us, larger shells—invisible until they burst—were hurtling through the night. They burst with blinding flashes, and with dull muffled thuds that shook the aeroplane and hurled me hard up against the side or top of my turret.

"I'm going to turn round and run over the target again," I heard Leonard say to Taffy.

Still the shells stayed with us and seemed to be, if anything, increasing. I began to sympathize with the pheasant who flies down the line of guns, being fired at by each gun, and still continues on apparently unscathed. But I knew how many are not really unhurt but drop dead or mortally wounded some distance further, and I wondered if we were like that and would do the same.

I began to feel rather lonely and cut off from the others, and wondered what was happening at the other end of the aeroplane. Perhaps even now they were clipping on their parachutes, preparing to jump . . . perhaps they had already jumped and forgotten all about me.

Almost as if he had been reading my thoughts Leonard said, "How are you, Revs?"

From that moment on, Leonard has always called me 'Revs'. Why, I have no idea, as most other people call me 'Riv'.

I managed to croak back some sort of reply. Those four words bucked me up no end. I felt again that I was not the only person in the aeroplane, and once more felt part of the crew. I wondered how the others were feeling, and if they were taking it as a matter of course.

I was still firing bursts at the guns and searchlights, and had a look at my ammunition. It would not do to use all my ammunition here; I should have to leave some for possible attacks by fighters on the way back . . . that is, if there was to be any *on the way back*. I wondered how we had got off free for so long, and felt the next one would surely bring us down.

Once again I heard Taffy give his lefts and rights. I wished he would hurry up and drop the bombs so that we could get clear away from all this. I had no idea how long we had been diving and twisting about in this fountain of fire and steel, but it seemed like all night. It seemed we had always been doing this and would always continue to do it.

Once more I heard Taffy say "Bombs gone" ... and thought 'Thank God for that!' I looked hard, waiting and hoping to see them burst. Suddenly, in amongst the flashes, I saw what looked like a sheet of flame ... and in the midst of the flame, blue and white flashes like lightning. Those flashes continued for several seconds, and completely outclassed the gun flashes.

At last we were clear of what Hell must be like, and were flying normally once more, and I heard Leonard say, "Someone bring me some coffee." I felt I could do with some, too: my throat and mouth were dry and my turret was full of the fumes of burnt cordite from all the rounds I had fired. I also noticed that my clothes were sticking to me with sweat. Once more we were flying undisturbed through the night, and once more I realized there was a moon, and felt a sense of tremendous relief.

I heard a banging against my turret doors, and put my hand behind my back to open them. There was Stokie with a flask of coffee and grinning his hardest.

"We've had enough for one night," he shouted in my ear, and I hoped he was right. I saw the Dutch coast on our return with very different feelings from those I had had on the way in, and was not at all sorry to see it disappear into the darkness.

It was just getting light when we landed and examined our plane from the outside. The wings, tail and fuselage were full of holes, and we counted over a hundred of them.

I went to bed after my first 'operational breakfast', but did not stay there for long as I found I could not sleep: flashes and bangs accompanied me whenever I started to doze off. Evidently Leonard had not been able to sleep either, for I found him in the ante-room writing letters. That afternoon we went to York to see *Top Hat*.

Two nights later we went right down to the south of Germany, to Leuna, and were flying for nearly eleven hours. The next trip was to Dusseldorf, then Essen, Duisburg, and so on. . . .

CHAPTER IV

THEN came the full moon period . . . and Cologne. I far prefer
operating when there is a moon: you don't get that enclosed
and rather oppressed feeling that you get on dark nights when
for the majority of the time you can see nothing but stars,
and sometimes not even them. We had a new wireless operator,
in place of Stokie, who had been posted.

When we crossed the Dutch coast I could see every detail,
with the sea looking like silver; stopping suddenly as it reached
the mud flats, and then dividing up into hundreds of little
glistening streaks as the moon glanced on the dykes and drains.
Sometimes I saw what looked like lakes but were, I imagine,
floods.

We saw the Rhine perfectly, winding and curling about,
and Leonard followed it for some time: it looked so serene and
quiet in contrast to all the flak being pumped up at us. I
thought what a rum game it was: all the hundreds of shells
being hurled up at us while we were waiting to send a load of
bombs hurtling down. Taffy must have been having some
trouble with his intercom. or something, for Leonard kept
asking him where we were, but could get no reply.

The flak suddenly closed down, and I heard Leonard say
something about a trap . . . probably fighters. I was watching
out very hard, but could see no sign of any fighters. It was
brilliantly clear, and I should certainly have seen them if there
had been any near.

Taffy must have done something about his intercom., for
I heard him talking to Leonard. We were too far north, so
turned south. All the time I looked about me ready for fighters
. . . which I did not see. It was certainly very quiet, unnaturally
so: we must be practically over Cologne . . . but not a gun:
only ourselves and the brilliant moon. The moon was to one
side of us, and I could see it by leaning forward and turning
round: I wondered how far I could really see . . . certainly
several miles. Leonard was cursing some low cloud, and I
looked down and saw it like white fleece below us.

Suddenly the world seemed to stop . . . or else race ahead!

24

I remember a deafening explosion and a blinding red flash which seemed to be inside my head and behind my eyes. I was falling through darkness . . . falling to the ground . . . I felt I was still in my turret, but could not see it; everything was dark and silent and the engines had gone. I knew we had been hit, and I imagined the shell must have burst somewhere behind my turret and blown it from the aeroplane . . . and I was falling in it! So this was the end! But it was not the end yet, as I was still falling. I wished it would hurry up and finish; it took so long. I had been falling for such a long time and everything was so quiet and I was all alone. Should I feel when I hit the ground? I must be nearly down by now, surely! If only I could see! . . . But no, I would rather not see . . . I would rather it ended quickly and not know about it.

"Revs! . . . *Revs!* . . . Come forward, Revs!"

So Leonard was here too! . . . but how did he get here? He was in the front! . . . *Come forward, Revs. . . .* What did he mean, *come forward*? . . . There was the moon, but it was red instead of silver. What were all those coloured lights? Hell! . . . they were shooting at us. Flak . . . always bloody flak! Why hadn't I hit the ground yet? . . . but I was not falling any more, and Leonard had spoken to me: he said *"Come forward, Revs."* I could not leave my turret unless he told me to . . . and I wanted to leave very badly: I was frightened and wanted to see someone and feel someone.

We were still flying and the engines were running. I put out my hands and felt for the sides of my turret. It was still there . . . yes . . . and whole. . . . I must go and see what had happened.

The door behind me was shattered to splinters . . . and there were smoke and flames, too. I must do something quickly. Leonard had called me forward, and he wanted me. I crawled forward through the smoke and flames.

God, what a mess! The fuselage door had gone, and most of one side of the fuselage as well. Desmond was there, working like a maniac, with his blond hair shining in the light of the flames, and his eyes sparkling like brilliants: sweat was pouring off his face, and he was hurling flares, incendiaries, and spare ammunition out of the gaping fuselage. I started to do the same . . . and he shouted at me to go back and get my parachute, as the aeroplane would probably break in two at any moment. 'Very probably,' I thought, and wondered how it was holding together even now. I hoped it would not give way before I had time to crawl back for my parachute. Somehow the idea of jumping did not worry me a bit; it seemed inevitable that we should have to do that . . . and it would be so simple just to fall out over the side. I hardly noticed the flak, and was only dimly aware of the crumps and flashes all around us.

When I got back to the fuselage with my parachute the flames had nearly all disappeared, but the place was still dense with smoke. I worked with Desmond until the flames had completely gone, and then went forward. The wind and slip-stream was whistling through the fuselage and tore at my clothing as I crawled along. Leonard was sitting at the controls, and turned round and smiled as I entered the cabin. Davy was sitting by his set fumbling for the morse key: his face was charred and black, and his clothing all burned. I looked at his parachute harness and examined the straps. If he had to jump I thought they would probably hold, as the flames had done little more than scorch them, although the surrounding material was nearly all burnt away. Davy looked very bad: he did not look as though he could pull the ripcord on his own, and I started to think out plans for getting him out safely.

It was almost as draughty in the cabin as it was in the fuselage, and I tried to get Davy to lie down on the floor, where it was slightly warmer, but he would not leave his set. Once I forced him to lie on the floor, but all the time he struggled to get back into his seat, and at last I had to give way to him. His one idea was that he must carry on with his job and not let us down. He had been standing in the fuselage by the flare-chute, ready to drop a flare, when the shells burst. A splinter from one touched off one of the experimental flares we were carrying; it exploded with a flash of several million candle-power . . . and how it did not blow him to bits or hurl him out of the fuselage—which was split and left with an enormous gaping hole down one side—I cannot imagine.

Poor Davy was very badly burned—chiefly about the face —and was quite blind. Desmond had fetched the first-aid kit and covered Davy's face with the jelly used for burns. It was bitterly cold in the cabin, and for the next five hours we did all we could for Davy's comfort: I kept putting his fingers in my mouth and breathing hard on them to try and get them warm. He kept asking me where we were. When we were still over Germany I told him we had crossed the coast and were over the sea . . . and when we were over the sea I told him we were over England and would soon be back. He must have thought the last part of the journey took an interminable time!

It was a nightmare journey, that . . . with the five of us crammed into the cabin of the Whitley, hardly ever speaking, and wondering how far we should get. Leonard was sitting at the controls; he had taken his helmet off, but was still wearing his yellow skull-cap, which looked grotesque in the half-light. Taffy was sitting at his navigation table grinning to himself most of the time: Taffy always grinned under all conditions! Desmond, looking like a wild blond giant, was part of the time sitting beside Leonard and part of the time looking at Davy. Davy sat at his set, hardly moving; I was crouched in the confined place beside him. As I watched his face I tried to remember what he looked like before, but his charred black mask gave me no help.

The journey back seemed endless, but, like everything else, it did end. We crossed our coast in broad daylight, and after landing were surrounded by an inquiring crowd.

I did not go to bed, but went into York with Leonard and Desmond. We went to a cinema again in the afternoon, and I slept through most of the show.

.   .   .   .   .

A few days later I was sent on a Turret Course, which lasted a week. When I got back Leonard told me he would shortly be leaving the squadron and going to a Halifax squadron. Naturally, I wanted to go with him, and he said he would try and fix it. I also did all I could to get posted with Leonard, but without any luck at all.

When I finally knew for certain that I should not be going with him, I set about to get myself fixed with a new crew. Desmond had been given a crew, so I asked him if he would have me as his gunner. I think he was genuinely pleased with the idea, but he said he was fixed for a gunner for his first trip

—which was that night—but would take me next time. There was not a *next time*—as Desmond was killed that night.

There were no more crew vacancies, and I had a spell with practically no flying. I was made Flight Gunnery Leader, which meant a certain amount of work on the ground—chiefly organizing. I wanted to get back into the air, and was impatient with this spell of inactivity.

CHAPTER V

AND then came Cologne again. I can't say I was altogether looking forward to this particular target, as the last time I went there we had the incident of the exploding flare, although I was longing for another trip. Incidentally, the last time I went there was the last trip I had done. I was to fly with a new captain, who was our flight commander, and a very decent chap. His pet remark was "God bless my soul!" . . . which always came out when he wished to show astonishment.

I had been acting as adjutant for the last few days, as our adjutant was on leave. I hated the job, as it meant being tied to the office with no chance of flying, and anyhow I knew very little about it.

We knew we were on by ten o'clock, and had plenty of time to do our Daily Inspections and Night Flying Test in the morning. We landed from our N.F.T. by twelve o'clock, and were free until briefing, which was at three o'clock. I am always restless before a trip, and can't settle down to anything, and find it difficult to concentrate: if I play a game of tennis or squash I find it very difficult to keep my mind on the game; I feel as I do before going to the dentist or before the beginning of a match.

The group gunner leader rang up during the morning to ask if he could fly in 'S', which was our aeroplane. 'S' had been given to the squadron by Ceylon, and as he had been in some journalistic job there before the war he wanted to fly in her and write an article on the trip for Ceylon. I was delighted when Andy said I was flying with him, and that he would not change his gunner: although, as I said, I was not particularly looking forward to the trip, I would not have missed it for anything.

There is a thrill and pride of achievement about operational flying that I can't describe. I feel at the end of a trip that I have really done something; that I have accomplished something great. I feel that I have defeated something, too, I don't know what it is: whether it is my own fear . . . or death . . . or what . . . but I always feel at the end of a trip a wonderful sense of calm and peace. I have always loved England, but never as much as I do when I return from a trip over enemy territory. There is always the feeling before setting out that it might be the last trip; that one might be blown to pieces or have to bail out over there. I don't think I am afraid of dying, but I am afraid of being taken prisoner and I certainly have a terror of being badly wounded, but, worst of all, I am afraid of being captured. It is the uncertainty of it all; not knowing how much longer I should have to be there . . . and wondering all the time what would be happening at home and who would be there when I got back.

I hate to see caged animals or birds, although we are told they are happy as they have nothing to fear and have regular food. But surely fear with an animal is an instinct without which it would have no self-preservation. Fear with us is not an instinct, but something very real, and something never to be forgotten. Some people have never known fear, except possibly by what they call 'a fright'. Real fear hurts: it possesses your whole being: it grips you and makes you conscious only of yourself: it makes you lose count of time! The coward in me sometimes says, '*Well, if you are taken prisoner you will have nothing more to fear. You will be safe, even if you are not at home.*' But no! I would rather fear . . . and live my own life and be surrounded by all the risks and uncertainties of war.

Briefing was longer than usual, as some of the crews had not been to Cologne before. It was to be a big effort, and our target was on the east of the Rhine: there were enlargements of our target maps, chalked in colours, on the blackboard. I studied these very carefully, noticing particularly the shape the river made as it curved through the town. I wanted to have a mental picture of this map, as sometimes you get a view from the tail that the others have not seen. The Met. report was not too good: the winds were high, and there was the possibility of a front before reaching the target. However, the Met. man held out good hopes of Cologne itself being free from cloud.

After briefing, we had tea, with a couple of boiled eggs. I was not feeling hungry, but I ate all I could; partly to keep warm, and partly because I did not know where or when the next meal would be forthcoming. After tea, I went to my room to put on some warm clothes.

I always wear as many clothes as I can: there is no excuse for feeling really cold in the air provided plenty of clothes are worn. It is often impossible to keep warm, but there is a great difference between feeling cold and feeling unbearably cold. The nose and tail turrets are the coldest positions in an aeroplane, and gunners usually wear more clothes than the remainder of the crew. I wore vest, pants, shirt without collar or tie—the latter a precaution in case we came down in the sea, as a collar is apt to shrink and strangle one—three pullovers, a roll-top sweater, and four pairs of socks, in addition to tunic, flying clothing, and scarf.

Before leaving my room I had a final check up to see that I had not forgotten anything. Pockets empty of all papers. (This, by the way, is an order, not merely a precaution, and is intended in case one is taken prisoner). Revolver . . . torch . . . pipe . . . tobacco pouch full . . . thermos flasks of hot coffee . . . extra scarf and gloves . . . money . . . clasp-knife . . . matches . . . these are the essentials I always carry. As I filled my pockets I tried to keep my thoughts steady: a lot of imagination can be a curse. My mind had to be free and clear for the next few hours; it would have to be quick and alert. All my movements while I was getting ready were intentionally unhurried: I had plenty of time, and there was no need to hurry. I did not want to feel rushed and flustered: I knew that I had to sit still for several hours, and a last-minute rush would not have helped. We were due to take off at 18.50, and at about five o'clock I set off leisurely towards the crew-room, where other air-crews were arriving with their kit.

The atmosphere in the crew-room before an operational trip is always exciting and tense. Everyone is jovial and friendly and seeming to give of his best, but all the same there is a feeling of strain, and one wonders how much people are acting. However, we are on the job now, and personal feelings do not matter.

While we were getting into our flying kit, the C.O. came in with the Station Commander. They, too, were more friendly than usual, and stayed talking to us until we were ready to move out to the aircraft. We had another five minutes before we needed to move, so we gathered into our respective crews and talked over again the plans of flight.

As I said, I was flying with the flight commander. He was

a very experienced pilot, although this was only his fourth or
fifth trip. He was fairly new to the squadron, so I did not know
him very well, but what I had seen and knew, I liked. He was
about twenty-three, but looked older: he had black hair and
black moustache, and large dark eyes. Our wireless operator,
Arthur, had actually finished his tour of trips, but had asked
particularly to fly on this one as 'S' was his old aeroplane.
His pilot had been posted, and he was waiting to be sent on a
rest. He was nineteen, tall and very cheery: he gave the
impression of being casual and even lazy, but when there was
a job of work to be done that concerned him he was always
there. He was an excellent wireless operator, and I knew he
could be relied upon in an emergency. Our navigator, Bill,
was well on the way towards the end of his tour; he was short
and fair and always grinning; he, too, was thoroughly reliable.
The second pilot, Martin, was new to the squadron; this was
to be his first trip. He was rather shy and quiet.

It was time to move out to the aircraft. The transport was
waiting outside the crew-room, and we piled in with all our
belongings: parachute packs, maps, Verey cartridges, thermos
flasks, and so on. I was beginning to sweat under all my layers
of clothing, in spite of my leisurely movements. The ground
crew were waiting for us by the aeroplane, and helped us
stow our kit.

It was still light, so we could see comfortably what we were
doing. I gave a final polish to the perspex round my turret
before climbing in. I sweated even more getting into the
turret, which was a hell of a job, clothed as I was. However,
I was in at last, and had a final check up inside. Everything
was as I had left it in the morning, and seemed O.K. My parachute and flask of coffee were stowed in the fuselage, just
outside the turret: I could reach both by opening the turret
door at my back and stretching behind me. Inside, I had an
extra scarf and gloves, chewing gum, chocolate, barley sugar,
biscuits, and clean rag. I put on my helmet and plugged in
the intercom.

The engines were being run up and tested: the whole tail
shook and vibrated, and the ammunition rattled in its tanks.
The ground crew were standing by, watching: one stood too
near the slipstream and had his hat blown off . . . it was rolling
over and over behind the aeroplane, and he was chasing it. He,

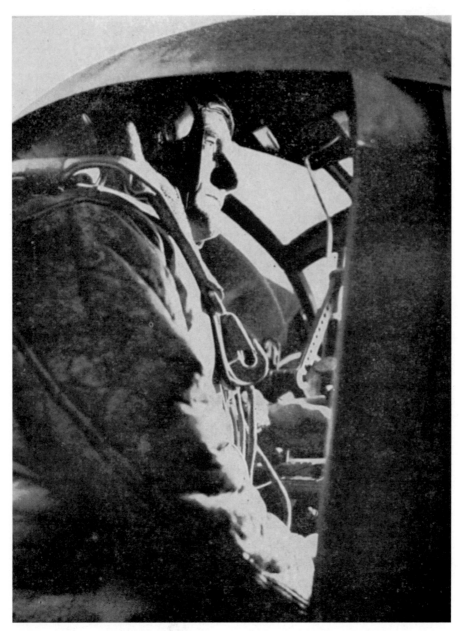
The author in the rear turret of a Halifax.

Revs, Brown, Taffy, Hares (extreme top), Jacko, Weldon, Cheshire and Gutteridge (centre bottom), No. 35 Squadron, Linton-on-Ouse, spring 1941. *Imperial War Museum CH6372*

The author and Leonard Cheshire in the summer of 1941.

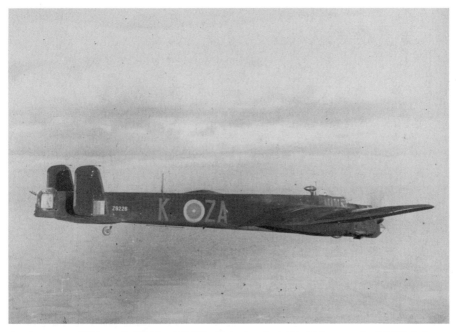

An Armstrong Whitworth Whitley Mk V in flight, late in 1941. This example, Z9226, belongs to No. 10 Squadron. *Imperial War Museum CH4450*

Two Handley Page Halifax Mk II, Series I's of No. 10 Squadron in formation over the Yorkshire countryside during 1942. *Imperial War Museum CH4433*

Whitley Mk V, T4261, S for Sugar, was the aircraft in which the author and his No. 102 Squadron crew, captained by Squadron Leader C.E. Florigny, ditched in the North Sea returning from Cologne on 1 March 1941. *Imperial War Museum CH2052*

A scene of activity at Driffield in 1940 with Whitleys of No. 102 Squadron. *Imperial War Museum C927*

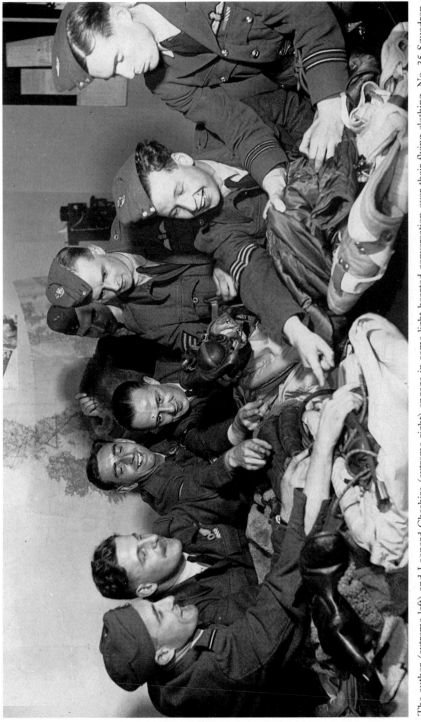

The author (extreme left) and Leonard Cheshire (extreme right) engage in some light-hearted conversation over their flying clothing. No. 35 Squadron, Linton-on-Ouse, spring 1941.

Flight Lieutenant Leonard Cheshire DSO, DFC, with his air and ground crew in front of their No. 35 Squadron Halifax, *Offenbach*, Linton-on-Ouse, summer 1941. *Imperial War Museum CH6373*

Inside the rear turret of a Whitley showing the four Browning machine guns, ammunition belts and the gunner's turret traversing controls. *Imperial War Museum CH686*

The sting in the tail of a Whitley: four .303-inch Browning machine guns in a Nash and Thompson power-operated turret. *Imperial War Museum C924*

Pilot Officer Leonard Cheshire's damaged Whitley Mk V, P5005, showing the extensive damage caused by a flare exploding inside the fuselage on their run-up to the target, Cologne, 12/13 November 1940. *Imperial War Museum CH6374*

too, was being blown along by the slipstream, and when he had retrieved his hat he had to struggle to one side, leaning forward until he was clear. A large pool of water by my turret was being thrown up into a fine spray, and some bits of oily rag were flying about in the air. I noticed all these things in detail as each engine was being run up separately.

My mind was absolutely clear. I no longer felt an individual, but somehow part of a scheme, working almost automatically. All day I had been preparing for this moment, and now I was ready. I could control my actions, but I could no longer control what happened to me. I must sit and wait. I was in the hands of my pilot . . . and God . . . and must sit and wait. I don't think pilots realize or appreciate the trust their crews have to put in them. Four or more men are literally under the control of one man: upon his quick actions and thinking depends largely their safety. If a pilot says "Jump," the crew cannot say "Is it necessary yet?" but must jump. It is not so bad when you know nothing about flying, but when you have flown and understand the principles of flying, you find yourself at times apt to criticize the actions of your pilot. This, I know, is wrong, as he obviously knows more about his part of the job than the remainder of the crew, but nevertheless it is so. A good captain of an aeroplane will not criticize the actions of his crew unless he knows them to be wrong. He will check up, yes . . . it is his job to know what each member of his crew is doing—the captain of an aeroplane is as much in command of his aircraft as a naval commander is in command of his ship.

Many people cannot understand how a sergeant can be in command of officers in his crew. Rank in the air, in a sense, does not count: the sergeant as captain of an aircraft is captain because of his experience and skill as a pilot. It has been decreed, and rightly so, that the captain of an aeroplane should be the pilot, and not the navigator, wireless operator, or air gunner. It is obvious, then, that as each squadron has a certain number of N.C.O. pilots, a captain will often be of non-commissioned rank, and may sometimes have one or more officers in his crew. Some of the best captains I have known have been N.C.O.s.

We were now ready to move off. Andy called through the intercom. and asked if I was O.K. and ready to move. I heard him call up each member in turn.

I liked the sound of his voice: it was clear and calm, and confident. Again, I often wonder if pilots realize how much the sound of their voices down the intercom. can mean to their crews . . . particularly that first call-up. Some pilots do it merely to check the intercom.; others to make certain that each member of the crew is in his position; but others, and these are the ones I like, call through in such a way as to make you feel personal and of some importance: they make you feel that your comfort and feelings matter and are of importance to them. Andy gave this impression, and I liked him for it.

He turned the aeroplane on to the perimeter track. The ground crew ran round out of the way of the slipstream, and watched anxiously and with pride. There were fitters, riggers, electricians and armourers there. They, too, had been working hard all day preparing for now: they had done their work and done it well. Each man there had a responsible job, and knew that the safety of the aeroplane and the lives of the crew depended to a great extent on how he did his work. They had taken a pride in it, and knew it was O.K. They were free now, but were in no hurry to go. They would watch us off the ground and out of sight before they went to their tea. As we moved away they gave us 'Thumbs up' and waved. I moved my guns up and down in reply: they were beautifully smooth, and I knew I could rely on them.

As we moved round the track we passed airmen who stopped and waved. Some were on bicycles and got off. Many of them were probably envying us, and wishing they had the opportunity to share our experiences.

When we reached the take-off point we had to wait our turn, and others were lining up behind us; it was beginning to get dark, and I could not see who they were. I again checked over my turret. Guns loaded . . . sight O.K. . . . loading toddle in stowage position . . . spare sight bulbs. Yes; everything was as it should be. We moved slowly round ready for take-off. I could just see a group of people watching us: there was the station commander, C.O., padre, duty pilot, and several others. They would stand there until the last plane was off, and then move off to their several jobs or relaxations.

The engine roared as the pilot opened the throttles with the brakes on; I could feel the tail beginning to lift as the aircraft strained against the brakes. We moved slowly at first, and then very rapidly. The tail was well up and there was a swaying movement as the pilot kept her straight with his rudders. The ground streaked past and seemed to be dropping; the watchers disappeared into the dusk below. We passed over the edge of the aerodrome, and I could see the lights glowing red and yellow.

As we climbed, the ground appeared darker and the colours faded. The light up where we were was brighter, which, by contrast, made the ground appear darker than it really was; but my job was not to watch the ground: enemy fighters have been known to lurk over the aerodrome and wait for the unwary crew.

A few months previous to this we lost an aeroplane and crew this way. They had taken off and climbed to about five hundred feet, when a Jerry fighter attacked them from the beam. The first the crew knew was that tracer bullets were hitting them in the fuselage and wing. One engine was hit and caught fire, and the aeroplane crashed in flames about a mile from the aerodrome. The only man saved was the captain, a boy of twenty. I met him a year later at a dance, and his nerve was still gone; although he was flying as an instructor he told me he did not feel equal to flying on operations again for some time.

It is pitiful to see a boy's nerve broken. Anyone whose nerve has gone goes through hell at times, and the cause of their breaking comes before them more vividly than at the actual time. The shock at the time of an accident is usually felt afterwards, and is not necessarily noticed at the time, but at the recurring memory when the imagination has had free time to work, the mind goes through all the mental torture that the imagination can conjure. Physical pain is quickly forgotten; but mental anguish brews and returns until it is almost stifling. A boy's mind should be free and gay, and should not know these horrors, but the mind of a boy who has tasted war is no longer young, but has outgrown his body.

We were still circling the aerodrome and climbing, and it was getting lighter instead of darker the higher we climbed. The ground appeared as a sort of grey-green colour, and seemed very remote and unreal. The aerodrome beacon was flashing red, and I made a mental note of the letters—'A.R.'

I knew we were still over the aerodrome, as I could see the perimeter and obstruction lights below, but that was the only indication of its whereabouts. Hangars and buildings had merged into the ground, and were invisible.

It seemed strange to think that life down there would be going on just the same. In the watch office they would have chalked up our time of take-off, and would be awaiting news of us on our return journey. In the Mess, people would be drinking their cans of beer, and talking and laughing and listening to the wireless . . . and some would be playing billiards or snooker, or table tennis. There would surely be a pair on the squash court, as this was the popular time for playing . . . and others would be going to York or Harrogate or Ripon for the evening. All these things seemed very far away. . . .

Up here we were five men working together and for each other, and we were all working for the same purpose: to reach Cologne, identify and bomb our target—doing as much damage as possible—and reach home safely. Our lives depended on each other, and each one of us was indispensable. The captain's job was to fly the aeroplane to Cologne and back and make a safe landing, avoiding flak and searchlights as best he could. The navigator's job was to tell him what course to fly, and to do this he had to calculate and check. Winds are his chief problem: he has to know the exact strength and direction of the wind at whatever direction he is flying. The wireless operator's job is to keep a listening watch at his set: he may be required to send out messages, or to help the navigator by getting loop bearings or fixes, but the majority of his time is spent listening. The second pilot sits next to the captain . . . and usually just sits! If the visibility is good he will probably map-read. He may fly part of the way. He is there to learn, and will be watching and noting all that goes on. My job is to keep a continual look-out for enemy fighters; to report on the movements of searchlights and positions of flak bursts; and to act generally as the driving mirror for the pilot.

"Just turning on the course now, Navigator. . . ."

I heard Andy say this down the intercom. and could see the lights of the aerodrome dead below us. We were on our way now, and were still climbing. The sky above us was a green-blue, and the western sky was lit by a glorious red sunset.

The red glow tinted the edge of my gun barrels and the perspex round my turret a bright red colour.

I was thrilled with the beauty, and called through to Andy, telling him about it and asking him if he could see it. He replied that he could just see the edge of it. They would have lost the sunset from the ground by now, but up here it was as vivid as the ground was obscure. On the ground one is not always conscious of the transition of light to darkness unless one's attention is attracted to it by some phenomena such as a bright sunset, or unless one is trying to race the light in a car. But in the air one is in the change; it is all around one. There are no shadows or trees, or hills, or houses to hasten the darkness: the light is about one and seems to linger as it changes colour across the sky, dawdling its way to the west, and sinking lower and lower until it shows only as a faint glow or streak on the horizon.

I had to keep my eyes moving: it does not do to have one's gaze fixed too long in one spot, as one is apt to get dazed and, anyway, the rear gunner's job is to search the sky and not gape at sunsets.

The stars were beginning to show as the sky grew darker. It was impossible to see now where the sky ended and the ground began. The sunset was fading, and there was just a yellowish glow left above the bank of clouds . . . which a few minutes before had seemed alive and glowing and were now a hazy purple-grey bank in the distance. It was as though our last link with the ground had disappeared: we seemed more alone than ever.

There was silence down the intercom. Our work was only just beginning, and we had plenty to think about without having to speak . . . and, anyway, there was nothing to say.

The sweat on my body was cold and uncomfortable, but I should feel more comfortable when it was dry. I took off my gloves and unwrapped a piece of chewing gum to chew . . . and wished the peppermint taste would last longer! I did not keep my gloves off for long, as it was beginning to get cold. I called through to the captain and asked the temperature: —10°. This, by the way, was Centigrade. Yes, it was going to be cold tonight, devilish cold. We should soon be needing oxygen.

The second pilot said he could see the coast line ahead . . .

and a few minutes later he said he could definitely pin-point us. The captain and navigator had a natter as to whether they should alter course now or wait a bit! They decided to wait. Bill said he thought we might be a bit out to the left. Good old Bill! . . . he certainly knew his job. He had got the winds taped, but to make sure he asked Arthur to get him some loop bearings.

I could see the coast line now, a thin light grey streak disappearing into the darkness below, and I tried to imagine what the coast would be like. It was a stretch I did not know. I wondered if the tide was in or out. The waves would be breaking on the sand, and I also wondered if anyone could hear us. They probably could, and might even be talking about us: some people were probably wondering if we were Jerries, and might be arguing if it were possible to tell a Jerry by the sound. I began thinking of people I knew, and of those at home. They would soon be having supper, and were probably listening to the wireless. They did not know I was up here, and I was glad they did not know, as they would probably be worrying . . . but it made me feel more alone, knowing they did not know. I felt sorry for those with sons and husbands and friends flying, and wondered if it was better for wives to live near the camp with their husbands and know when they would be flying, or to live away from the camp and not know when their men were flying. On the one hand they would have the certain knowledge that their men were out on one particular night, and would be free from anxiety on other nights; but, on the other hand, those living away would never know the night their men were flying or were free, and would have the continual strain of uncertainty.

The coast had disappeared, and all that was visible was a misty grey blanket below us with some lighter patches which were clouds.

Martin took over, and did not fly as steadily as Andy: I could see the stars moving slowly backwards and forwards across my perspex as the course altered. Andy told him to watch his course. We were about ten thousand feet up, and I turned on my oxygen supply. I told Andy I had done so, and he said everyone else had better do the same. I at once began to feel warmer and more comfortable. Oxygen acts on you very quickly: you can be feeling cold and drowsy one minute . . .

and almost immediately after breathing more oxygen you feel perfectly normal.

I once took an oxygen course. Besides being given various medical facts and formulæ about oxygen, we were shut into a decompression chamber to test out under the various atmospheric conditions the effects of oxygen and the lack of oxygen. There were six of us in this chamber, which was a large cylindrical structure with chairs and tables inside. Round the walls on the inside were the oxygen plugs and dials exactly as fitted to an aeroplane. From the face mask on your helmet you have a long rubber tube, about four feet long, which you plug in to connect with your oxygen supply. There are two dials near this connection—one marked off in *thousands of feet* and the other showing the contents of your oxygen bottles. When you want oxygen you turn on a tap which releases the supply and at the same time the flow is registered on the dial which is marked in *thousands of feet*. You turn the tap until the needle registers the same number of feet as the height at which you are flying.

Well, we were all sitting round the inside of this iron cage with our oxygen turned on, while the pressure was brought to the equivalent of *twenty-five thousand feet*. We were each of us given something to do. One man was reading *Punch*; two were writing; two were doing simple sums in arithmetic; and I had a V.G.O. machine-gun connected electrically with an illuminated target. The target was in the form of a screen, with twelve discs illuminated from behind by electric bulbs. The discs lit up individually and remained illuminated for four seconds, during which time I had to sight them in turn and fire. If I sighted them correctly a bell rang. If not, nothing happened until the next disc showed after four seconds. It was perfectly simple, and I was able to do it every time on my trial go.

The object of this demonstration was to show us how the individual behaves without sufficient oxygen. We were all of us accustomed to the use of oxygen, having used it many times in the air. The effects of insufficient oxygen are similar to those of too much alcohol, and people are affected in different ways. Most people become over-confident, and some become argumentative; but in all cases their reactions and movements are slowed down and slurred although they may be feeling fine and very confident.

The man who was reading *Punch* was the first to be experimented upon. At a signal from the doctor—who was watching us through a glass panel from outside—he turned off his oxygen and continued reading out loud. He carried on normally for a few minutes, but soon his reading became slower and his speech slurred. He got worse and worse and started repeating himself. The rest of us were in fits of laughter. He was ludicrous, an apparently drunken man with nothing to drink! After a short time the reader became inaudible and started convulsions, and the paper slipped from his twitching fingers as he fell sideways off his chair on to the floor. At this point the doctor signalled us to turn on his oxygen for him. We were by this time more interested than amused, and I think each of us was wondering what we should be like when our turn came. I know I was! After our patient started breathing oxygen again we helped him back on to his chair, giving him back his paper and his actions were more or less reversed: he started reading again, at first slowly, but gradually regaining his normal stride. Now, the curious thing was, he had no idea he had even faltered, let alone passed out; and he would not believe us until he saw exactly the same thing happen to the next man! Each of us did more or less the same thing, only some were funnier than others. I was told I started off shooting normally, but gradually got worse and worse until I was not shooting at all. When my oxygen was turned on I slowly improved until I got back to normal again. I had no idea I had been anything but normal!

At the end of the course all of us swore we would be very much more careful in the use of oxygen in future . . . and would see that those with whom we flew were the same!

·   ·   ·   ·   ·

"What is our E.T.A. at the Dutch coast, Navigator?" Andy asked.

"Just a minute, sir, and I'll find out. Another seventeen minutes, sir," was Bill's reply.

"Thanks. Is everyone feeling all right? How are you in the tail, Riv? Feeling cold?"

"Not too bad, sir. I can't see much, though."

"No, it's pretty nasty, isn't it? It looks as though the Met.

were right. I hope they're right about it clearing over the target."

Below was a uniform grey which looked like dirty cotton wool. We kept flying through cloud which rushed by us as a damp grey haze, making the inside of the aeroplane even darker; it was rather like going through a tunnel in a train. As we passed through these clouds we bumped and tossed like a ship on a rough sea. Above us was even more cloud, with only occasional clear patches through which we could see the stars. The inside of my turret was coated in frost, and my oxygen mask was frozen stiff and chaffing the bridge of my nose: I kept on lifting it and tried to put it back on a fresh spot, but each time it slipped back to its old place. I could see about an inch of ice on the top of my gun barrels, and I had to keep working my turret every few minutes to prevent it freezing up. It gave me something to do, and also helped me in my continual search of the sky. We were not likely to meet any enemy fighters in these conditions, but it would not do to relax.

On the outward sea crossing one is always more alert and awake. The job is only just beginning, and one has the antici-pation of what one is going to see or meet, but on the home-ward journey, if all goes well, one is apt to have that feeling of a job done and the worst over, and to tend to relax. Also one is tired, and it requires more effort to keep alert. A night-fighter pilot once told me that he usually experiences far less opposition from returning enemy bombers than from those who have not yet dropped their bombs.

We were nearing the Dutch coast, although it was impos-sible to see it. We hoped to be able to pin-point ourselves when we picked up the Rhine—if we were lucky enough to do so. It would be maddening if it was a wasted effort, and we would not be able to see anything, after all!

Bill said he could see some searchlights through the clouds some distance ahead, so we were near the coast, if not actually over it. I felt a sort of tension as I always do when over enemy territory. Anything might happen now!

Yes, we were definitely over the coast: I could see a glow through the clouds which was obviously searchlights. The clouds did not look as thick as I thought they were. I could see some heavy flak bursts away out to our port, like jewels sparkling: I wondered who were up there, and if they were being hit. It was not a heavy barrage, and was either being fired at more than one aeroplane or was inaccurate, as the points of light were at different heights and dotted about the sky. Whoever was up there would be giving them a spot of annoyance and trouble below . . . which was something, anyway! Also a hell of a lot of money being spent sending up those shells . . . and, provided they did not hit anyone, money wasted.

We were flying at fifteen thousand feet, and the temperature was —30 degrees Centigrade. I was cold but not uncomfortably so. My brain felt slightly numb, and it was an effort to concentrate, but all the time I felt a sort of inner excitement which prevented me thinking about my physical discomforts. They did not matter, anyway, as I was not there to be comfortable! If I had been comfortable I should probably have fallen asleep. I could feel no sensation of movement except when we were being bumped, which was fairly often.

There was the monotonous noise of the engines, which sometimes seemed to change their note. I wondered if the noise really changed, due perhaps to varying atmospheric conditions, or if the changed note was only in my imagination. Maybe it was something to do with the pressure on my ear drums.

Sparks from the exhaust pipes were continually showering behind like sparks from a bonfire in a wind. They, and passing clouds, gave me the only impression of speed. Sometimes they came with a burst, as if they had been held back and suddenly released; and on several occasions I involuntarily started and realized with a shock that my mind must have been wandering.

Surrounded as I was by this grey expanse of cloud and ice, and sitting with perspex and metal within a few inches of me all round—unable to move save only my arms, and with the roar of the engines so loud that I could shout without hearing my shout—my mind felt as enclosed as my body. A few hours ago I was free and walking, and could see people and hear them talk! But now, although there were four men within a few feet of me, their existence felt as remote and unreal as my own body felt. I was conscious of time: one has to be in the air, as accurate navigation is based upon precision of timing. My thoughts were the same. I was conscious of the cold and my own discomforts . . . not that they worried me; they were part of the job. I could think of my home and my friends . . . of leave . . . of games . . . but most of all of the job in hand. My eyes continually searched the sky—not vaguely, but intelligently and with method—and my hands still worked my turret, while all the time my thoughts ran free and seemed to keep pace with our own flight through the air.

I realized I was still chewing on the same piece of gum that I had started on shortly after leaving base. I unwrapped a fresh piece and exchanged it with the old one: it was frozen so hard that I had to melt it in my mouth for some time before my teeth would make any impression on it.

The weather seemed to be improving and I could see stars again . . . also a few searchlights which were playing about on our port. I could see them through the cloud, which was not very thick here. They moved slowly through the air, white shafts of light feeling their way about searching for a victim, like some giant octopus seeking its prey. My spirits rose as the weather cleared; it did not look as though our venture was to be in vain after all.

Some searchlights suddenly came up from below, where apparently there was no cloud. They seemed to be mostly from behind us, so I called through to Andy, but he had already seen them, as the aeroplane leaned over and felt as if it was dropping through the sky. I realized then that Andy must be flying again, although I did not remember noticing the change-over. As the aeroplane leaned over on its turns the searchlights seemed to come at us from our own level instead of from below, and to be swinging round. They next looked as though they were falling underneath us and coming up the other side. One of them swung on to us and stayed with us. Gosh! how bright it looked! Every detail of my turret showed up, and I felt I wanted to hide! How huge the aeroplane felt! . . . and no longer remote and alone. There were men below—and possibly near us in the air, too—seeking to destroy us: we were their enemy, and they were using their power for our destruction.

The aeroplane continued its antics; diving and climbing and swinging about the sky. I was very much alert now, and strained my eyes against the blinding whiteness of the light. A fighter might or might not be near. Anyway, we were a well-illuminated target, should there be one about, and I certainly did not intend him to have a sitting shot ... *and I did not intend him to have a shot at all if I could see him first!*

There was complete silence down the intercom., as we were all too intent to speak. It was as though we had been disturbed by a rude visitor, and one that we wished would go! Two more searchlights were on us now, and held us despite all Andy's antics. Suddenly I saw a shape above us! It was the silhouette of an aeroplane! Instantly I swung my guns up, but almost immediately realized it was our own shadow projected on to the clouds above us by the searchlights below.

They went out as suddenly as they had appeared, and we were left in complete darkness—a darkness even darker than before—and I realized I had been sweating despite the cold.

Andy straightened the aeroplane out and continued on his way. I continued staring into the darkness and still chewed my gum.

"Well, you've seen some Jerry searchlights now, Second Pilot," said Andy.

"Yes, sir."

"I think that must be our target ahead, Navigator. There's a hell of a lot of heavy flack going up."

"Yes, sir. I was thinking the same thing. It's about where it should be."

"Good! I'm going to climb some more before gliding in. All that stuff looks about our height."

"O.K., sir. I think I'll go forward now to the bomb sight." This last was from Bill, as he was going to drop the bombs.

As Andy opened the throttles wider for our climb, a more vicious shower of sparks shot behind.

I began to feel very excited. The big moment had nearly arrived. We were near our target, and soon we would be trying our hardest to identify it. We had had a very clear description from the intelligence officer at briefing, and knew just what to look for, and I could still see that chalked map in my mind's eye. We were over Germany ... over the country with which we were at war! Below were our enemy; the people we were trying to destroy.

Up there the air was the same as at home. It was cold and clean, and unless we were being fired at there was no difference between flying here and flying over England. A few hours ago we *were* over England, over the country for whose freedom we were fighting and whose people we were trying to save. Although we were over Germany, all we could see was a grey colourless mass with occasionally a few lights, and sometimes some very bright lights which were searchlights, and some flashes which were guns. Those guns were trying to destroy us . . . and we were trying to destroy the material and men and women that made those guns—and the guns that fired the shells. It was to be a race for one side to succeed. Our skill was pitted against their skill.

"When we get there I'll circle round before going in. See if you can identify the target, Navigator. When you do we'll go straight in . . . we've got plenty of time."

"Right, sir. Another five minutes ought to see us there! Shall I drop one stick?"

"Yes . . . drop one stick if you get a good run-up. If you don't get a good sight, we'll come in again. . . ."

I was staring out into the darkness. It was a temptation to look at the ground, but a temptation that had to be overcome, as the danger of fighters near the target area is always great.

"Yes, that's Cologne all right," Andy said. "I can see the river. God bless my soul! Look at all those flares! We're not the first by any means. There are several fires already."

We were circling round the outskirts of the city, and I could now see what was going on. By jove! what a sight! As Andy had just said, we were by no means the first. I could see three or four large fires glowing red, and several specks of red which must have been more fires just starting. There were dozens of searchlights: some appeared stationary, some were waving about the sky, while others intersected at one point. Those I knew held a victim, although they were too far off for me to see him. Those that were weaving about formed intricate patterns against the sky.

There were bright yellow balls floating gently down: these were flares dropped by other aeroplanes. They were at all heights, and by the light of those nearer the ground houses and streets could be seen quite clearly. The river Rhine could be seen, too, as a bright silvery streak winding through the town as the water reflected the light from the flares. Flashing across the ground were bright yellowish-white flashes, which were guns. The flashes were continual and were jumping here, there, and everywhere; whenever I looked down they were flashing and leaping about . . . while every few seconds there were brighter and bigger flashes which I knew to be bombs bursting.

There must have been an unholy din down there, though up in the aeroplane there was only the roar of the engines and our own voices down the intercom. There was plenty to say now, and we said it. In the air shells were bursting with their jewel-like flashes . . . and tracer shells were streaking up like brightly coloured snakes writhing about the sky. What a sight! Lights everywhere! Beams of light, streaks of light, flashing lights, white lights and coloured lights, searchlights, shells, bombs, fires and flares . . . all at once: hundreds of them all darting about and jumbled together, shooting up and flashing . . . while way up above the stars shone but were forgotten.

"I've got it, sir! No mistaking it." Bill's excited voice came down the intercom. "If you turn to the left now you'll see it."

We turned to the left and Andy closed the throttles. The contrasting silence was a relief as we made our gliding approach over Cologne. I could see brilliant flashes followed by black puffs of smoke as shells burst on either side of us, but they were too far off to do us any harm. The turmoil was all around us now, but was not directed at us; we were approaching unheard and unseen, and seemed to be spectators high up in some gigantic arena watching this display of fire and fury. Above us . . . below us . . . in front and behind . . . shells were bursting in a thunderstorm of steel! Searchlights in their dozens were streaking the sky, while tracer shells popped up in their snaky path like little balls of light chasing each other in their climb to the sky. Their upward journey got slower until at last they could go no further, and fell down in a gentle curve and then exploded.

"Left, left . . . steady! . . . Left! . . . steady, steady . . . steady . . . Left! . . . steady. . . . *Hold it!* Steady. . . . Steady. . . . *Bombs gone!*"

Bill almost screamed the last two words. His excitement was infectious, and I peered down, straining my eyes against the glow below.

"Can you see the bombs from the tail?"

"No, I can't see the bombs; there are too many flashes. But I can see the incendiaries, though."

They were white and very bright like white Neon lights,

and were spreading across the ground. Ours were not the only ones: they seemed to be everywhere. Many had already found their mark and had turned into red glowing masses, and I hoped ours would do the same. There were many more fires now, and they were getting bigger.

We were still gliding silently, and so far had not been touched. We were weaving slightly from side to side, thereby lessening our chances of being picked up or hit. As we banked on our turns the ground, with all its turmoil of lights and flashes, appeared to tilt from side to side. Andy must have been enjoying himself, and was probably muttering *"God bless my soul!"*

When we were clear of all searchlights and flak, Andy opened the throttles: the engines roared their noises again, and sparks shot out behind.

I felt elated and wanted to sing. What a trip! . . . and what a wonderful view! If only all trips were like this one. I had forgotten about being cold or uncomfortable, and my heart went out to Andy. By his skill and planning he had brought us safely away from Cologne and danger. I did not mind admitting to myself that I had been dreading Cologne again, but I could laugh at all my forebodings now. This would be a trip worth remembering . . . and the sort of trip Leonard would have enjoyed. I felt as though I had really done something, though I had done less than anyone, being merely a spectator, and had just sat.

My joy and high spirits were due partly to the tremendous feeling of relief at the easiness of the trip, as much as to its success. All the forebodings that my imagination had been conjuring up had been in vain. We had left Cologne unscathed, whereas last time we came away wounded and sore. We had seen far more than we had expected to see. There was none of that uncertainty and doubt that one sometimes has on the return journey, wondering where the bombs really fell. Our object had been achieved: we had definitely seen and bombed our target.

I looked at my watch. I would time the flares and note how long I could see them. I had often read in the newspapers '. . . and the fires could be seen twenty minutes after leaving the target'. Well, we had been flying for fifteen minutes, and I could see them very clearly. There was a bright red glow on the horizon which tinted the sky above it a wonderful warm red. The glow was still and steady, but every now and then was brightened by sudden flashes as bombs continued to burst—probably increasing still more the fierceness of those fires. The searchlights were less bright from this distance, and could just be seen as pale silvery streaks which seemed to stay stretched across the sky. The flak bursts were still sparkling and flashing.

I was reminded of the sunset we had seen on leaving our own aerodrome, and thought what a fitting description it would be for the fires I could see . . . *and twenty minutes after leaving the target fires could be seen glowing like a sunset.* That was just how they looked, and I must remember to mention that at interrogation.

"Have you sent the 'Off target' signal, Wireless Operator?" Andy asked.

"Not yet, sir. The wireless has gone for a burton."

"D'you think you can fix it?"

"I'm trying to sir. I've got it in bits. . . ."

"Right! Let me know how you get on. Do you think we are on track, Navigator?"

"I don't know, sir, but I hope so. I can't see a bloody thing!"

"No, neither can I. With any luck we shall be able to pin-point ourselves when we cross the coast."

We were passing through some sort of electrical storm. Blue flames were running up and down my gun barrels. The flames did not seem to be coming from the barrels, but to be dancing round and round, and up and down, hardly touching them. The trailing aerial also seemed to be alight with a blue flame running its whole length. I was fascinated, watching this flame that did not burn, and I called through to Andy to tell him about it. He said the same sort of thing was happening round the airscrews as well.

It was now forty minutes since we had left the target, and there was still a faint red glow away out on the horizon where Cologne was. I could no longer see any searchlights or flak, but occasionally there was a brightening of the glow as bombs continued to burst.

Arthur called through to say the wireless was still U.S., and that there was nothing he could do about it. He had tried everything but could not get a squeak. If Arthur could not do anything, then no one could in the air! Andy said we should have to do without it, then; an obvious remark, no doubt, but he did not seem to be showing any concern about it.

We kept on flying through misty clouds, and I could hear the ice cracking on the tail plane and fuselage like pistol shots.

"We should be getting near the coast soon," Bill said. "Our E.T.A. is in another seven minutes."

There was nothing to be seen—not even searchlights. My excitement had died down, and I was once again conscious of discomfort and the cold. I was beginning to feel very sleepy, too: my eyelids felt heavy, and I had to strain to keep them open. I began saying the morse code through to myself to keep awake. . . . *What were our beacon letters? 'A.R.' . . . dit-dar, dit-dar-dit.* . . . It would be waiting for us . . . *dit-dar, dit-dar dit.* . . . They would be waiting for us in the watch office and ops. room, too. They would probably be getting anxious, not having heard from us as yet.

"Can you see anything from the tail, Riv?"

"Not a blooming thing, sir!"

Arthur asked if he should drop a flare, but Andy said it was no good as there was ten tenths cloud below. There was nothing to show us where we were. However, every minute that passed meant we were so many more miles nearer home. . . . I must not forget that bit about the flares being like a sunset.

We continued on our way, bumping now and then, and the minutes ticked by. The engines seemed to take on the sound of our beacon . . . *dit-dar, dit-dar-dit.* It was as though the engines were calling to the beacon as a horse neighs when it nears its stable.

We could not say for certain where we were; we might be over the land or we might be over the sea. There was no indication from below: no lights, no signs of land or water . . . only cloud. There was nothing we could do about it, either. We had come down to four thousand feet, and there was still cloud below us. The pilot had got his course from the navigator, and was steering it; we knew our E.T.A. for the English coast, which was in about another seven minutes, but that was all.

Arthur was still working on the wireless set, but said it was pretty hopeless. We could only just sit. Bill could do nothing more, either: he had worked out his course and knew his

E.T.A., but without aid from the wireless or without seeing the ground he could do nothing more. Andy was flying with the aid of his instruments, and Martin was sitting beside him, while I was still in my turret, looking out into the darkness and feeling very cramped and sore in the bottom.

Our E.T.A. was up, but whether we had crossed the coast we could not tell. We carried on. Suddenly we saw a flare path below us: there was no mistaking it, and I think we all more or less saw it at the same moment. There was just a small break in the clouds through which it was visible. We circled and came down through the clouds to below one thousand feet. Andy said he would land there, although we did not know which aerodrome it was, as we could not see the beacon. We rather felt it was 'a bird in the hand'.

It is always rather an anti-climax landing at a strange aerodrome, particularly when one is tired. It usually means a long wait until daylight or until the weather improves before being able to get home. During the last part of a trip I always look forward to that cup of tea and a pipe before interrogation . . . followed by a jolly good breakfast, and then, best of all—bed! True, at a strange aerodrome one gets the cup of tea, pipe, and breakfast . . . but not one's own bed.

Andy was bringing her in now, and I prepared myself for the bump. Not that I mistrusted Andy's landing, but I had had too many bruises not to be careful.

At the last moment, and almost too late, they gave us a *red*. Andy opened the throttles fully, retracted the undercarriage again, and we climbed and circled once more. We saw the sea now for the first time . . . *and it was on the wrong side of us!* There was no mistaking it. The sea was on the north-west. Surely we could not have crossed England? . . .

We continued in a wide circuit, with all of us peering at the ground. I had forgotten all about fighters. There was the sea again! This time on the south-east. Where the hell were we? We all knew but could hardly believe it: this was one of the Dutch islands!

We did not waste any time. Andy turned the nose in a northerly direction and kept the throttles open, and Bill got really busy. He had got his pin-point! Our feelings were of relief and amazement. Who was the mug who had given us the red? That we shall never know . . . and it still puzzles me.

It seems incredible: a British bomber would surely be recognized a few feet above the aerodrome, even at night . . . but
instead of enticing us in they had actually warned us off and
never fired a shot. They must have had a mug on duty that
night, and thank God for it!

At any rate we knew we were over the sea now, and Bill
said he recognized the island: he gave Andy a fresh course to
fly, and had some pretty ripe remarks to make about the winds.
Andy asked for a new E.T.A. for the English coast, but Bill
said he had no idea, as the wind had completely altered: it had
blown us about a hundred miles off our course, and was dead
against us.

We could see the sea quite easily now. Even at a thousand
feet and in the darkness we could see the waves breaking into
white horses below us.

Andy said we were getting very low in petrol, and unless
Bill was wrong about the wind we would probably have to
come down on the sea. We had enough petrol for another
twenty minutes' flying . . . and about eighty more miles of sea
to cross. There was nothing that he could do, except go on
flying and fly as economically as he could: it was a question of
getting as near to our own coast as we could before coming
down.

I don't think we quite realized our predicament even then.
We had been flying for about nine and a half hours and a lot
had happened in that time—and we were still far from being
out of the wood.

The fires would still be burning in Cologne, where there
would be a lot of suffering and misery. That is what we had
intended. Our target had been a large factory, and a lot of
night-shift workers would have been working there: there
would be people dead or dying, there would be people burned
there. Some might be alive . . . living with broken bones,
unable to move, and with crushed and mangled bodies pressed
against them . . . with nothing but the stink of rubble and
putrefying flesh for company. There would be people with
arms and legs blown off . . . and people with their stomachs
blown open . . . and people with half their faces blown away.
They might have to wait hours or even days until they were
found; unable to help themselves and wishing they could die
. . . yet afraid to die. Some would be badly burnt and would

die: others would not die, but would be crippled and scarred always. All these things I had seen when our own aerodrome was bombed.

While all this was going on we were flying away from the havoc we had caused, and would soon be near death ourselves. We were near death now, but how near we could not know. We might, or might not, make a safe landing . . . and even if we did, we might, or might not, be rescued. We would do all we could, the rest was in the hands of God. Every second we were getting nearer home; and the nearer home we got, the greater were our chances of being saved. We had no wireless, so could not send out an S O S.

Had any of our Radio Direction Finding stations picked us up? And were we being plotted yet? Upon this depended largely our chances of being rescued. If we were being plotted we definitely had a chance: if not, we had practically no chance at all. Still, there was nothing more we could do except wait: we were still flying and we were still alive!

I had a definite and active job to perform now, as Andy had put me in charge of the dinghy party. My first job was to hack away the fuselage door.

The fuselage light was on, and I could see what I was doing quite easily. There was not much room to use the axe and, hampered as I was by the confined space and all my clothing, I soon began to sweat and labour. Yet all the time I felt a sort of satisfaction in chopping with the axe: I felt as a child might feel who had been told he could break his toys instead of being told he was not allowed to! The door came away quite suddenly and was whisked away by the slipstream . . . and I nearly went with it!

My next job was to see that the dinghy was ready for launching, and I wished I had taken more interest in dinghy drill! The dinghy was on the fuselage floor just aft of the door, and there was a long cord leading from it and tied to the fuselage. I made certain that this cord was firmly attached; as it not only acted as the rip-cord for inflating the dinghy, but was also the only means of securing the dinghy to the aircraft.

I called through to Andy to tell him that all was ready at our end and he replied that he could carry on for a bit yet. I leaned out of the doorway as far as I dared, and had a look below. The sea was rough, devilish rough: I could see the waves breaking over each other in the darkness. There must have been a hell of a wind blowing.

Suddenly I saw a light, and called through to Andy to tell him, but he had seen it too, and was turning round to investigate. It was quite bright, and was on the water, but what it was or where it came from I had no idea: whether it was on a ship, lightship, buoy, or what. Arthur suggested dropping a flare, and Andy agreed . . . but we were not high enough for the flare to be of much use, as it touched the sea almost as soon as it ignited, and went out. Arthur launched one after the other, but all with the same result: they lit up for a second and showed the sea in all its fury—but no sign of the light or from whence it came. As soon as the flare hit the sea it smouldered, and I could imagine the sizzling sound it would make . . . and then darkness. The light was still there, and Andy decided to come down as close to it as he could.

Bill gave me the Verey pistol and some cartridges, which I put inside my flying suit, and he, Arthur, and Martin did the same with the other cartridges. We now took up our positions ready for the crash-landing.

Martin and I were lying on the floor right by the open doorway, with our feet braced against what we call the step, which is a raised part of the fuselage about two feet high and just forward of the door. The other two were sitting on the step with their feet by our feet: they had their backs towards the front, and we had our feet towards the front . . . and we were all hanging on to ropes slung from the roof.

We were coming down now, and hanging on for all we were worth. Andy throttled back and we braced ourselves even harder: he must have held off too soon, as he opened up again and then throttled back in a few seconds.

There was a terrific crash, and the lights went out. We were hurled forward and drenched with icy water, and completely blinded by the darkness, which was intensified by the sudden change from the light. We struggled to our feet with the water above our knees and the waves crashing against us through the doorway.

I groped for the dinghy and hurled it through the opening. I was holding on to the rip-cord and could feel the dinghy inflate . . . and I was surprised at the speed with which it did so. I heard someone shout—*"Quickly, sir!"* . . . and felt the drag of the dinghy against the rope in my hand as I hauled it towards the aircraft.

The rope suddenly became slack. It had broken! I hurled myself into the sea and felt the dinghy with my hands. I did not notice the cold. The dinghy was being hurled and tossed about like a cork . . . and I, too, with it, as I was washed across it.

Arthur and Martin were there, too; I think I pulled them on top, but Bill was still in the water, and I had hold of him by the arm. God! what a weight he was! I was kneeling and hauling on Bill as hard as I could, and shouting to the others to help: Arthur half gasped and half shouted back that he could not, as I was kneeling on top of him. So I was! Poor old Arthur. He struggled from underneath me and got a hold on Bill, who was a dead weight and nearly drowned. Martin had hold of his other arm, and I had hold of his clothing round his shoulders. He was kicking with his legs and imploring us to pull him with us.

We *had* to get him aboard: that was all I could say or think. We must not lose him . . . we could not leave him. He was a living body: we were alive . . . *and he must live, too!* The waves were breaking over us furiously, and we were being hurled about unmercifully, but still we kept our grip on Bill, and still we hauled. I was using all my strength, and was hopelessly out of breath. Several times we had him nearly with us, and each time a wave hit us and we fell sprawling and almost into the sea, but still we kept our hold. Arthur, Martin and I on the dinghy, and Bill in the water . . . and Bill was drowning and we were getting weaker. *O God . . . give us strength!*

The waves had washed us on board, so why should they not do the same for Bill? We began to wait for the waves, and when Bill was lifted so we pulled . . . and at last—and after how long I have no idea—we had him with us! Bill lay gasping and grinning on the dinghy with us!

There were four of us huddled together and hurled about . . . *but there should have been five.* I think Arthur was the first to voice our thoughts, but up to now all our energies had been on Bill: we had him in our hands, and by our efforts we saved him. But Andy . . . Andy was not with us.

We could now see better, and we saw him. He was fifty yards away, standing on the fuselage of the sinking aeroplane—

We could see him standing on the fuselage of his sinking aeroplane

the aeroplane in which he had saved us—and we could not save him. There he was alone and waiting. We saw him when we rose with the waves . . . and lost him when we went down with them. All the time we were getting farther away . . . and all the time his aeroplane was sinking.

What could we do? The answer was, *nothing* . . . absolutely nothing! We could only watch and thank God for our own lives: we had no paddles, and no one could swim in a sea with waves higher than a house. We did not know if Andy had seen us. We shouted . . . but our shout was blown back at and behind us. I don't think he heard our shout, and I don't think he had seen us.

We watched Andy. We watched him disappear with his aeroplane . . . and were silent.

There were four of us, and we were alive. We were in a sorry plight, but we were alive! We were drenched and at the mercy of the fury of the waves, and the wind was howling against us . . . with the tops of the waves blown up into a spray and dashed against our faces. Our faces stung, our mouths were filled with water, and our eyes smarted from the salt. We were sitting round the edge of the dinghy with our feet in the middle. We realized by now that the dinghy was upside down . . . with all our comforts and provisions underneath and by this time washed away!

There we were sitting on a circular rubber surface about four feet in diameter, which undulated and moved with the weight of our bodies and the rise and fall of the waves. I could feel it writhing underneath me like a live thing.

We could still see the light with its reflection on the waves, and guessed it to be about half a mile away, but still we could not tell what it was or where it came from. I got out the Verey pistol, which was already loaded, and fired a cartridge.

The coloured stars shot up, and we could see each other clearly by their light: they fell in a curve into the sea, and I noticed and was thrilled by the colour and beauty of their reflection in the water. The sea sparkled and shone with all manner of brilliant lights and colour, which suddenly disappeared as the stars were drowned.

I fired three cartridges altogether, and we looked and waited to see what we might see, but we saw no answering signal from a ship or any sign at all. We saw the brightly coloured stars as they soared up and floated gently to the sea, and the brightly lit sea heaving and swirling about us and breaking into white clouds of spray . . . but there was no reply or sign from the light.

We seemed to be part of the waves, and were drifting away from the light. Where a boat would have been dashed to pieces, the rubber dinghy merely gave in to the waves and took its shape from them: they could not break it, and they could not sink it. The dinghy fitted to our bodies and we stayed with it. We could not hold on, as there was nothing on which to hold . . . but our bodies were relaxed and we leant and swayed with the waves, fitting the rhythm of our movement to the heaving of the water.

We were still exhausted from our exertions with Bill, and we were sprawled, half-sitting and half-lying, round the edge of the dinghy with our legs tangled in the middle. I looked at my watch, which was withstanding the water and was still going.

It was five o'clock. We sat and stared at each other and listened to the sea. Martin was sick: he turned his head and vomited with the wind, his whole body heaving. Poor Martin . . . he felt worse than the rest of us: this was his first trip . . . and what a trip! He was still dazed and bewildered, but he was taking his hardships marvellously.

Our weight in the centre of the dinghy made a sort of saucer-like depression which was filled with water, so that our legs and feet were immersed. The sea had soaked through our clothing and boots, and it was abominably cold. . . .

We must bail the water out. But how? . . . I took off one of my boots and tried with that, but the leather was so soft and flabby as to be useless. We each had our caps in our pockets, and we tried using them: they proved quite good for the job, and by holding them open with both hands we scooped the water up and threw it over the side. Only two of us could work at this at once . . . and when the two nearer the direction of the wind tried throwing the water over the side, it merely blew back again. None of us was doing much good, as the waves continually replaced what water we threw out, but at least it gave us something to do and helped us to keep up our circulation.

I think that first hour was the worst. There we sat in the

darkness, shaking with the cold and just able to see each other, being hurled up and down, and drenched by the waves which at times hit us so hard they took our breath away; the wind tearing at our clothing, stinging our faces, and smarting our eyes; unable to move or stretch our legs, which were across each other's and already getting numb with the cold.

It would have been easy—and it was a temptation at times —to drop back into the waves which seemed to be stretching up ready to receive us. It would have been over in a few minutes: a few minutes of struggling for breath and choking . . . then blackness . . . and whatever follows. As we were, what would be the end? Exhausted, numbed with cold until we could stay on no longer and were washed away by the waves? . . . or slow death from starvation and thirst? . . . or madness? I knew of one crew that had gone insane: they had been in the dinghy for three days, and then one by one had gone mad. But we might be picked up! There was always that chance, and we held on to it: it gave us strength and endurance. There was that will to live which is stronger than the wish to die. We were young, strong, healthy, and had homes and friends. We loved life and we wanted life . . . ah, dear God! we wanted life more than anything. What had we done in our young lives? Certainly not all that we wished to do. We had been in danger many times before, and near death, too; we had seen death . . . but death in others. Death for us was near now . . . but I don't think I was afraid. I do know that I wanted to live; to see my home and my friends. . . . I loved my home and my friends . . . and I loved life. . . .

We were very close together in that dinghy. Our bodies were touching . . . but it was more than that: we were sharing our lives, and I think our thoughts were the same. If we died we would die together . . . and if we were saved we would be saved together.

Our actions continued the same and became almost mechanical: throwing water over the side and keeping our balance on that heaving dinghy. We spoke very little: conversation was in our thoughts. We spoke of our homes and friends, but never of our discomforts; they were too real. We spoke of Andy, and asked each other time and time again how we could have saved him. How *could* we? I still ask myself that question, but have not found an answer yet.

I can still see him silhouetted against the sky and not moving, as we rose on the heights of the waves. Could he have reached us? No! . . . no man could have swum in that sea in flying clothing.

Bill had lost a boot in his struggling in the sea, and we tried to keep his foot out of the water . . . but there was nowhere to put it except on top of our own, and the waves wetted it then just the same. It was stiff with the cold, and he could not move it.

The dinghy was not spinning round, as might have been expected, as there was a canvas sea anchor which kept it straight. Arthur and I were with our backs three-quarters to the wind, with Bill and Martin opposite us. Bill and I did most of the bailing, as from our positions with the wind it was easiest. Martin was still retching, and was feeling terribly ill, but he never once complained. His retching and sickness made him very weak, and I knew he was feeling wretched. The waves were hitting Arthur and me on our backs and went down our necks, and were hitting Bill and Martin in the face. On the whole, I think Arthur and I had the better of it.

I still had the same bit of chewing gum in my mouth that I had before reaching Cologne. I suddenly became aware of it and spat it into the sea.

Our eyes had become quite accustomed to the darkness now, and we could see each other quite easily. Martin had slipped more to the middle of the dinghy and was half lying across it with the top half of his back, head and shoulders almost touching the sea behind him: in fact, many times he was submerged, but he did not seem to notice it. Poor chap, he was in a very bad way: when I spoke to him he did not seem to hear. Bill was sitting hunched next to him, and was pushing his cheerful face to meet the waves. When a particularly fierce one hit him he merely grinned, with the water dripping off his face, and all the while he was throwing water over the side. Arthur was leaning forward with his arms across his knees, and seemed more cross than anything. Bill and I had to time our scoops for water, as there was not room for both our hats in amongst our legs at the same time: our hands were stiff and painful with the cold and were already swelling, and I found it difficult to hold my hat.

At times I felt in the depths of depression and despondency,

and as if a heavy weight were on my chest. At these moments
I needed every ounce of courage I possessed to keep my body
composed. The others were probably feeling the same—I know
Martin was—and I hoped I was concealing my feelings as
successfully as they were. At other times my thoughts were
almost gay in comparison, and I felt a sort of thrill and
exhilaration in our wild gyrations: my spirits seemed to rise
and fall with the waves as they took us with them where they
would. We were never still: up and down . . . at times so high
it seemed we should be blown from the tops . . . at other times
so low it seemed the weight of the water must come down,
swamping and drowning us. But our dinghy, the most sea-
worthy craft of its size, was always on top.

So we sat and watched the waves get lighter, lightened by
the dawn which came with storm cloud and rain . . . while at
base they would have given us up by now and chalked up one
word—*Missing*—against our names. I had seen that word
many times, and had often wondered where those men would
be. They would be wondering about *us* now, back at base: we
were just one of those crews that *Failed to return*. . . .

Martin spoke for the first time, and said:

"When will they send telegrams to our next of kin?"

"Oh, when the old adj. starts work . . . not for another
hour or two yet, anyway . . . they always wait a bit to give us
a chance to turn up," I answered. "You're married, aren't you,
Martin?"

"Yes, sir . . . I'm married."

"Where does your wife live?"

"In the village. I live out."

"I expect the adj. or padre will go round and tell her,"
I replied. "Much better than having a telegram. I always think
a telegram is much too brutal . . . and seems final, somehow.
You'll have to cheer her up to-night, Martin."

"So you really think there *is* a hope, sir?"

"Good lord, yes! . . . of course I do! They'll be scouring the
water for us by now."

"I've got a date in York to-night," said Bill.

"I wish *my* girl lived in York," Arthur replied.

And all the time it was getting lighter. What should we see?
The sky got lighter and the clouds took shape: dark clouds
racing low across the sky and competing in fury with the

We sat and watched the waves get lighter

waves . . . waves as fierce as ever, but majestic in their beauty. We could see their colours now . . . colours changing all the time.

You can't describe colours . . . there are too many . . . any more than you can describe music. Music does not consist of single notes any more than colour consists of one colour: music is a harmony and rhythm of notes, while colour is a harmony and continual change of an infinite variety of subtleties of colour. You can say a thing is blue or green or red or brown: but there are hundreds of varieties of blues, greens, reds and browns . . . and some blues are so nearly green and some browns are so nearly red that the changes from blue to green, or red to brown, are so gradual that it is hard to say when blue ceases to be blue and becomes green, or when brown ceases to be brown and becomes red. So it was with the sea . . . never still, never the same . . . always changing in shape and colour.

There was no sign of ship or land. We were alone and waiting, and we wondered just where we were. Bill said he thought we were thirty or forty miles from our own coast, and we began wondering if we were on any shipping route. It was too early yet to expect help, as it was only just light, and they would not send out anything until now.

"I wish I had a cigarette!" Arthur said.

He brought out a packet soaked to pulp, and threw it into the sea. It was carried away and disappeared instantly.

We saw a speck below the clouds: it was an aeroplane flying towards us! We watched it excitedly and intently as it got nearer. I got the pistol out ready to fire: it felt heavy and awkward in my numb fingers. The aeroplane came nearer, flying fast and low . . . and we saw it had twin engines and a single rudder, so we took it to be a Blenheim.

I waited until it came nearer, and fired the pistol: I found the trigger hard to pull, and had to use both hands, my fingers were so weak. As I fired, Bill shouted. . . .

"*My God . . . it's an 88!*"

He was right; it was. Thank God it had not seen us, but carried on its way and disappeared into the clouds.

"He's been up to no good," Arthur remarked.

Very soon some seagulls appeared, apparently from nowhere.

They hovered around us, motionless in the wind, with only their heads turning from side to side.

"Let's hope they stay and bring some pals," I said. "A ship might see them if it can't see us, and guess there's something near."

It is amazing the way seagulls will appear when there is a ship or human being on the sea. They obviously hope for food. These gulls soon found they had come to the wrong place, and that we had nothing for them . . . and they continued on their mysterious journey—we knew not where. They had made us feel less alone, and had somehow given us hope.

I was struggling to reload the pistol, but the cartridges were soaked and swollen. Eventually, by peeling off some of the outer casing, I managed to push one home and close the breech.

It started to rain hard . . . and we leant back our heads and let the water splash into our faces and trickle down our throats. At first it was refreshing, but soon it became monotonous and uncomfortable as it poured down our necks, making us even wetter than before. We sat with shoulders hunched, and Arthur swore.

The rain did not last long, though, and the weather showed signs of improving. The clouds were lifting and there were some breaks in them: a patch of blue sky showed overhead, giving more colour to the sea. More seagulls kept appearing; some staying, and others flying past without taking any notice of us. I saw some gannets fly by, with their pointed wings and heads, on their straight course, just missing the tops of the waves: they seemed to be flying with more purpose than the other gulls. I love watching gannets, and even there I could watch them with interest and pleasure. There were oyster-catchers, too, chattering in their high-pitched voices as they passed with rapid wing-beats. I was surprised to see them so far out to sea, as I had always imagined them to be shore birds. Perhaps this meant that we were nearer land than we thought? I confided my hope to the others.

Again we saw an aeroplane approaching in the distance! There was no mistaking it this time, with that short fuselage and twin rudders. *It was a Hudson, flying about two hundred feet above the sea and about half a mile from us!* I struggled frantically to fire the pistol . . . but my fingers were so cold and stiff and swollen as to be almost useless. Bill was helping, and at last we got it off . . . but too late, as the Hudson was well past us and went out of sight. I had even more difficulty in reloading the pistol . . . and while I was still trying the Hudson reappeared, this time on the other side of us. I tried my hardest to load the pistol while the others waved frantically —but in vain! The Hudson disappeared.

I remarked that if there was one there would probably be others. We felt better. The clouds were lifting, and the sun threw its rays horizontally across the sea and dazzled us: the lights sparkled and danced on the broken surface of the sea that shone as brightly as the sun. The wind was still tearing at us, and the waves were still soaking us . . . and we were shaking with the cold . . . but we felt more cheerful with the light. I had never been so cold before. The others' faces were white and patched with blue, and I could see their teeth chattering: my own sounded like a roll of drums! My legs were stiff and painful and my back ached: I would have given anything to have been able to lie down. I tried to change my position and move my legs, but found I could not. I picked up one and moved it a few inches: the joints hurt abominably when I moved them, but I could feel no sensation in my leg at all. The only one oblivious of our surroundings was Martin, who lay back and stared upwards at the sky . . . and I am sure without seeing the sky.

"I wonder if she knows yet," he said.

"Will she take it very badly, d'you think?" I asked. I knew he was referring to his wife.

"I don't know what she will do. She's all alone."

"The adj. will look after," I said. "He's very decent like that. Anyway, you'll be with her yourself soon."

"I told her I should be back before dawn."

"Well . . . you'll be a bit late . . . but think what a welcome you'll get. It'll probably be worth it."

I did not like the look of Arthur. He had not spoken for some time, and his eyes were wandering round without looking at anything. He asked me the time.

"Getting on for nine o'clock," I told him.

"I can't stand another four hours of this! Have you got your revolver, sir?"

"No . . . I've lost it," I answered him. I was carrying it

Another view of the rear turret of a Whitley. *Imperial War Museum C913*

An armourer checks the four Browning machine guns in the Boulton and Paul rear turret of a Halifax. *Imperial War Museum CH6676*

Flight Lieutenant Leonard Cheshire, DSO, DFC. *Imperial War Museum CH9136*

Armourers bombing up a Whitley Mk V with 250 lb GP bombs. *Imperial War Museum CH680*

Two No. 35 Squadron Halifaxes over the French port of Brest on 18 December 1941. Smoke can be seen rising from the German warships *Scharnhorst* (top right) and *Gneisenau* (centre right). *Imperial War Museum C2228*

Wing Commander B.V. Robinson's Halifax Mk II, V9978, A for Apple, releases its bombs over Brest on 18 December 1941. The author is in the rear turret. Shortly after this photograph was taken the aircraft received a direct hit from flak in the port wing, badly damaging both port engines. *H. Mennell via C. Blanchett*

A No. 35 Squadron Halifax banks steeply over Brest. *H. Mennell via C. Blanchett*

With the port inner propeller feathered, smoke pours from the damaged port outer engine.

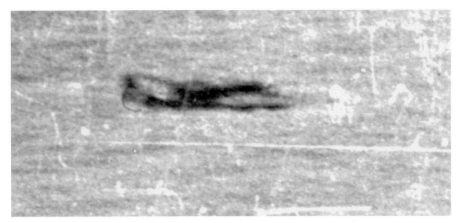

Both port engines are now out of action and A for Apple loses height quickly...

... hitting the sea in a plume of spray...

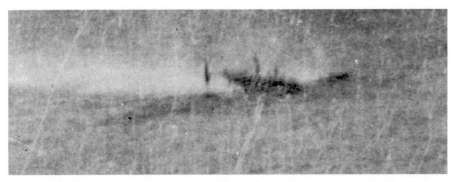

... and settles in the water. A for Apple remained afloat for forty minutes allowing all of the crew to evacuate the aircraft and take to the dinghy. They were picked up by a motor launch within three hours of ditching. *All H. Mennell via C. Blanchett*

Date	Hour	Aircraft Type and No.	Pilot	Duty	Remarks (including results of bombing, gunnery, exercises, etc.)	Flying Times Day	Night
					Time carried forward —	2203.5	39.40
18.12.41	10.00	HALIFAX II V9978	W/C ROBINSON.	OPS.	IN TAIL. TARGET SCHARNHORST AND GNEISNAU AT BREST. BOMBED TARGET IN LINE ASTERN FROM 10,000 FT. PERFECT VISIBILITY. BOMBS STRADDLED TARGET. VERY INTENSE AND ACCURATE HEAVY FLAK. DIRECT HIT IN PORT WING. BOTH PORT ENGINES HIT. LANDED IN SEA 60 MILES OFF CORNISH COAST AT 03.15. DAMAGED FOOT ON LANDING. HALIFAX FLOATED 40 MINS. F/O WILKERSON CIRCLED UNTIL 13.45. LISANDER SPOTTED AND CIRCLED US AT 15.00. PICKED UP BY ML DART AT 16.00. LANDED AT YARMOUTH AT 21.30.	03.15.	
					TOTAL HOURS DEC. DAY 12.15		
					TOTAL TIME ...	2223.50	138.40

The author's logbook entry for 18 December 1941: 'target *Scharnhorst* and *Gneisenau* at Brest'.

tucked in my flying boot, and it came out in my struggle on to the dinghy.

Arthur was trying to open the clasp-knife which was slung round his neck . . . but, thank God, his fingers were too weak from the cold for him to be able to do so.

"Don't be a damned fool, Arthur!" I said. "Go over the side if you like . . . *but you're not going to make a mess in here!*"

He began to laugh, and soon said:

"I'm sorry, sir."

"Nothing to be sorry about," I answered. "I knew you were only fooling."

"I *wasn't* fooling."

"Oh yes you were! Besides, what about your girl? She would have minded, you know."

"I told Mum and Dad I'd finished with operations," Arthur said a few minutes later. "I wonder what they'll do when they get the telegram?"

"Probably give you a good raspberry when you get back," I answered.

Our eyes were continually searching the sea: when we were carried to the top of a wave, Bill and I would stop our bailing and strain our eyes to the horizon. Our range of vision was very limited, though, as rolling, monstrous waves prevented us from seeing far. We did once see a ship when we were lifted by a particularly high wave . . . but only for a second or two, and then it was gone and we never saw it again. We tried to see if we were drifting in any particular direction, but there was so much movement all around us that it was impossible to tell.

"I wonder why they gave us that *red*?" Bill remarked.

"I can't imagine, but I'm jolly glad they did!" I replied.

"My gosh, so am I!" Bill said quickly.

"I wonder if I'll ever see my D.F.M.?" Arthur said after another silence.

"I didn't know you'd been put up for one," I exclaimed. "Jolly good show!"

"I'm not supposed to know, but Jimmy told me." Jimmy was his last captain. "Do you think we *shall* die, sir?" he went on.

"No, I don't think so," I answered. "No . . . I don't think we shall die. It'll be grand to look back on, though, won't it?"

"I'd rather not look back on it!"

The clouds were nearly all gone, and the sun was getting higher in the sky. The sea was not so rough, and we were not getting swamped quite so often. Our bailing was becoming of more use, too . . . but each time we got nearly to the bottom, a fresh wave came in and gave us more work to do.

"If this was peace-time and we were near the shore, we'd be paying money for this sort of thing," I remarked, after a long silence.

"I don't mind if I never see the sea again," Arthur replied.

"My home's by the sea," I told him.

"Where?"

"Cornwall. . . . D'*you* know Cornwall, Martin?"

"No, sir . . . I've never been there."

"You ought to take your wife there when you get leave: they're sure to give us some leave after this."

I was getting terribly weak and stiff in the joints, and it was becoming a real effort to throw the water over the side; both Bill and I kept stopping in our movements, and we were getting slower and slower. My legs were completely numb, and it was impossible to move them except by picking them up: on several occasions I picked up Arthur's foot, thinking it was mine! Bill's foot without the boot would be in a bad way by now. He said he had no feeling in it at all.

Arthur suddenly produced a small packet of chocolate, which he divided into four. We ate it greedily, in spite of the fact that we should probably feel more thirsty. Martin was sick again.

I looked at my watch. It was nearly eleven o'clock. How much longer could we last? We could last until dark . . . but I doubted if we would be able to see through another night. The last two hours seemed to have gone by very quickly.

"They must have sent the telegram by now!" Bill remarked.

"Yes, I expect they have," I answered. "It seems strange to think of what is happening at home. We know we are safe, but *they* don't. It's worse for those at home: if we die it's the end . . . but for them it's only the beginning. But don't let's talk of dying! It's only eleven o'clock, and there's bags of time for them to find us yet."

We began discussing and imagining how they would set about it. Would any of our own squadron be searching for us?

. . . Probably they would. The sky was quite clear of clouds now, and the visibility was good. If only the wind would drop! It did not give one a chance to get warm: it seemed to get right inside our clothing, and into our bodies.

Arthur had dropped forward with his head between his knees. I did not know if he were asleep or in some sort of coma, but I was glad. I hoped he would lose consciousness, and *stay* unconscious: if he had to go, I hoped he would not know the end.

Can you tell the moment of dying? If you are shot through the heart and die instantly, can you tell the instant of dying? Is dying like sleep? . . . oblivion? Do those who die in their sleep know any difference between their sleep and their moment of dying? Is there blackness for evermore? . . . or does your mind re-awake in a different body and different surroundings? . . . I began wondering these things. Should we know when we were dead? If we lost consciousness, would that be the end? . . . or should we know in our unconsciousness that we were dying?

Bill and I looked at each other, and each seemed to understand the other's thoughts: we seemed to gain strength from each other, too. We were still bailing water out, but very slowly, and we would continue to do so until our arms could no longer move.

Suddenly Bill said:

"*Listen!*"

"What is it?" I asked.

"Can't you *hear*? . . . an *aeroplane*!"

So it was . . . and a Blenheim this time, all right . . . flying about two hundred feet and zig-zagging about. *Oh, God! Make it see us!*

Arthur was alert now, and we all eagerly followed its flight with our eyes, turning our heads first one way and then another as the aeroplane changed its course. Its snaky course was getting nearer . . . very slowly, but nearer . . . as we watched it with alternate waves of hope and despair: turning towards us and then away again. It was very close now, and surely *must* see us. I had the pistol and was doing all I could to fire it . . . but I could not! The others tried, too, but with no better luck: our fingers just would not move.

And all the time the Blenheim searched, searched for us,

but did not see us. It was moving away now and had not seen us: it was still searching . . . but it was *going away*. . . . We watched it turning first one way and then another . . . but always away from us: we watched it going away, and we watched it until we could see it no longer. It had gone, and we were alone . . . and we felt more alone than before!

We continued to watch the sky when the Blenheim had gone . . . and we saw it reappear, still flying from side to side. It seemed to be making straight for us this time, and would surely pass overhead. It was getting very near now, and we waved our arms frantically. We shouted in our frenzy . . . as though the anguish of our shouts and minds must reach those men searching a few hundred feet away.

Ever nearer the Blenheim came, turning this way and that. Suddenly it turned and flew right around us, less than a hundred yards away. *It had seen us!* . . . and the crew were waving to us.

Can you imagine our joy? I don't think so . . . unless you have been facing death for nearly eight hours. We felt as a condemned man must feel who is reprieved on his way to the scaffold. I felt a surge of happiness such as I had never known before. Although our bodies were numb and stiff, our minds recovered instantly.

I looked at my watch. It was *eleven-thirty*. We had been in the dinghy a little over seven hours.

Our hearts were filled with joy, which showed in our faces. We had been found! We were not actually safe yet . . . *but we had been found*. We were no longer drifting aimlessly about the sea and getting weaker . . . but had been seen and were being cared for. We had been spotted, and were now the centre of focus of a vast organization working for our safety and home-coming.

The Blenheim would have wirelessed to its base, giving our exact position . . . the Navy and air-sea rescue service would be informed . . . and ships would be sent speeding to our rescue! We could look to the future now with joy, instead of with sadness and dismay.

We began speculating as to what would pick us up. Would it be a destroyer or a motor-boat . . . or would they send a seaplane? I knew a crew who had once been picked up by a destroyer. Could you get a hot bath on a destroyer? They would be sure to have hot meals . . . hot tea, hot whisky, and *a bed*! yes, a bed . . . perhaps, best of all, a bed . . . a warm, comfortable bed!

We could now think with pleasure of such comforts . . . whereas before we had not dared to speak or even think of them.

How long would it take for help to arrive? I guessed about three hours. We were already craning our necks and straining our eyes in the direction of the shore, looking for the ship to take us home, in the same way as people on a railway station look down the line for a train that is late.

Round and round the Blenheim flew . . . watching us; guarding us. We made a mental note of its number. We must write to the crew when we got ashore . . . go and see them and thank them. Had they any idea how we felt? . . . Could they possibly know of our gratitude and joy? How could they? To them we would be no more than just an unfortunate air-crew that had not quite made it: they would be glad that we were safe, but they could not be more than that. We were just four airmen whom they had saved, and they would be glad . . . but that was all. But to us they were as brothers: they had saved us when all seemed hopeless and lost.

We owed our lives to them. . . .

How could we let them know of our appreciation and happiness? They, too, must share our tremendous joy: they had made us happy, and they should know of our happiness. We waved to them, and thanked them in our hearts.

Bill and I continued our bailing . . . for some purpose now. Whereas before, our actions had been purely mechanical, now they were essential!

We noticed for the first time that the dinghy was not quite so buoyant and was slowly losing air. This caused us some concern: how long had it been deflating? The buffeting it had been having was beginning to tell on it, and there must be some tiny punctures or cracks. We tried to see where the air was escaping, but could see no signs of any holes. We sat as still as we could, hardly daring to move for fear we should make the leakage worse!

Some horrible thoughts began to haunt me. Suppose the dinghy was more damaged than we thought, and was ready to split! It would be appalling if it sank now . . . and we were drowned before the ship arrived. Until the Blenheim came it would not have mattered, but now it did not bear thinking about. The dinghy had had some terrible blows from the waves, which must have strained the rubber to its utmost endurance.

There was still a big swell on, and although the waves were only breaking over us occasionally now, the dinghy was being twisted and contorted continuously: there were great folds across the rubber, and I could feel and hear it chafing with every movement of the sea. How much longer could our little craft stand up to the strain . . . and how long had the Blenheim been with us?

Forty minutes. . . .

Pray God we could hold out until a ship arrived.

Bill suddenly exclaimed:

"I can see a ship!"

"Where? . . . Are you *sure*?"

"Yes. I saw it a few minutes ago, when we were on the top of a wave."

I turned my head in the direction towards which Bill was pointing . . . and, sure enough, when we rose high, I could see a speck in the distance which was obviously a ship. If it was really coming for us, it was coming far more quickly than we had ever dared to hope.

Bill kept watching it when we rose with the swell, and he reported that it was getting nearer, and that he thought it was a destroyer. Presently he said he could see two more. Magnificent! Three ships for four men!

We began discussing whether we should get leave . . . and how much. It was marvellous to be able to look to the future and make plans again: I could contemplate home and friends now without a pang.

'*What a lucky chap I am . . . and how good life is,*' I thought.

It was now possible to discern details on the ships as they came pitching and tossing towards us. We could not yet see what type of ships they were: they might be destroyers, or they might be some smaller craft, but what did it matter? They were ships, and they were coming for us . . . coming to take us home. Very soon we would be warm and cared for.

The Blenheim was still circling us, and evidently was going

to stay with us until we were aboard the rescue ships. Every second brought them nearer . . . and all the while our joy was increasing. No longer were we four destitute airmen . . . but four lucky men whom God had decided to save, and who had lives to live.

The ships were not the destroyers we originally thought they might be, but they looked like some sort of trawler. We could just make out figures on the nearest one. They were closing towards us very rapidly, and our joy and excitement knew no bounds. We started waving to them, but could not see yet if they were waving back. As the leading ship came within hailing distance, one of the men in the bows called out:

"Is anyone hurt?"

Then almost immediately on our reply that we were all right:

"Have you been seasick?"

As they drifted slowly nearer, questions and replies were shouted across the water. If our joy had been great before now it was terrific. If only Andy had been with us, life would have been perfect. . . .

Men were leaning over the side watching us, ready to help. One of them threw a rope across, which we managed to hold between us, and we were hauled alongside the trawler with our dinghy rubbing against its friendly hull. We were rising and falling with the swell . . . sometimes almost level with the deck, and at other times right down by the heel.

One of the sailors lowered himself down the rope ladder into the dinghy to help us in being hauled aboard: our legs were useless, and would not hold the weight of our bodies, so we could not climb the ladder, but by much pushing from below and pulling from above we were at last dragged aboard the ship and lay helpless on the deck.

We could only smile and thank our rescuers time and again. They put lighted cigarettes between our lips, gave us some neat whisky, and pulled off our flying clothing. They then helped us below into their cabin, where there was a roaring fire, and undressed us; we sat naked in front of the stove, absorbing the glorious heat, while the sailors raked out blankets, stockings, woollen pants and jerseys.

Very soon we were sitting round the table wrapped in blankets, with mugs of hot tea, glasses of whisky, and plates of bacon and eggs before us, talking and laughing and joking. Never before had life been so good . . . or people so kind.

Never shall I forget those men, rough fishermen used to daily hardships and dangers themselves . . . yet as kind and gentle as mothers. All our wants and comforts were attended to with the greatest care and thoughtfulness: our mugs of tea and glasses of whisky were never allowed to remain empty; we were given cigarettes and also some tobacco for my pipe; bunks were prepared for us . . . and we lay talking and smoking until we fell asleep, swaying with the regular roll of the ship.

Life was too good and full of interest for us to sleep for long, though. By sleeping we missed the full thrill and enjoyment of being alive! I kept reminding myself that I *was* alive, that there was still the future.

We told our stories time and again to fresh sailors coming to see us. We kept them plied with questions, too: how had they found us? Where were they taking us? Where had they come from? . . . and so on as the hours passed by: hours of happiness and relief.

When we neared port, and the time was approaching for saying good-bye to our new-found friends, we exchanged addresses, and wanted to give the skipper five pounds to split amongst his crew, as we could just scrape up that amount between us . . . but no, nothing would induce any of them to take a penny! All they asked for was a souvenir, such as a button off our tunics. I told the skipper to get busy with the scissors . . . which he did!

We slept that night in hospital, where incidentally I think Ming got more attention than I did . . . and before going to bed we telephoned our unit and homes to let them know that we were safe. To cut a long story short—and a still longer journey by rail and road—we arrived back at the aerodrome at about midnight on the following night. We had hoped to be allowed to go straight to bed, but on arrival we were greeted with a message to report to the Station Commander at the ops. room.

I glanced behind me just before going in, and saw Bill with a broad grin on his face.

"Don't look so damn fit, Bill, or you won't get any leave! Start trembling or something," I whispered.

Two days later we went on leave.

·   ·   ·   ·   ·

When I returned to the squadron from leave, I went to see the C.O. He told me that Bill, Arthur and Martin had been sent on a rest, and he asked me what I would like to do.

I wanted to know if my nerve had been affected, and the only way I could tell was to do another trip. Bill and Arthur had both done considerably more trips than I, and both needed and deserved a rest . . . but I felt I would like to go on longer yet. I asked if I could do another trip as soon as possible . . . and would the C.O. take me? . . . He said not that night, as he was already fixed with a gunner, but next time.

That night he and his crew were missing.

I put in another request to be posted to the Halifax squadron that Leonard was in . . . and, much to my surprise and joy, my request was granted immediately, and I moved the following day.

I arrived at a slack time for the squadron, and spent the period learning all I could about the new aeroplane. I had hoped to join Leonard's crew straight away, but for some obscure reason this was not to be, and I was put to fly with my flight commander, Braddles. He was a good pilot, but I was very disappointed not to be allowed to fly with Leonard again.

Both Leonard and I put in repeated requests that we should be together . . . but in the middle of our negotiations he was sent to America for three months. So that was that!

Braddles used to vary his crew somewhat, with the exception of Wheeler—his engineer—and myself, his tail gunner. Wheeler was a quiet lad of about twenty, and a first-class engineer. He was very quiet and precise in his movements. All his actions were deliberate, and he gave the impression that he would do nothing without thinking about it very carefully first. Even his smile, which started with his eyes, seemed to be carefully contemplated before it was allowed to appear.

The first trip I did with Braddles was to the Ruhr: then Magdeburg, Hanover, the Ruhr again . . . and so on. On several trips we carried the new four-thousand-pound bomb— a monstrous, ugly thing which looked more like an engine-boiler than anything else. When it was released, the aeroplane seemed to give a sigh of relief, and rise as light-heartedly as a lift.

On one occasion I missed this light-hearted feeling in the

aeroplane as the navigator said—*"Bombs gone!"*—and sure enough, a few moments later I heard him say—*"The bloody thing's still there!"* He tried everything he could to free it, but without success, so we had no choice but to bring it back with us.

Normally it would have been perfectly safe to land with it, but we did not know how near it was to dropping off. Also we had been hit by flak over the target, and we wondered if our wheels or under-carriage might be damaged. It was an unpleasant moment as Braddles made his approach for landing, but I consoled myself with the thought that if it did go off we should not know!

CHAPTER VI

A FEW days after Leonard got back from America—on July the twenty-third, to be accurate—Braddles sent for me. . . .

"I've some news for you, Riv," he said. "We're on a *daylight* raid tomorrow, and you're flying with me."

"Good show!" I replied. "D'you know where we're going?"

"No, not definitely, but we're after the *Scharnhorst*. She's left Brest and gone south, but I've not been told where yet. We load up here and go down to Oxfordshire, to a place called Stanton Harcourt, some time this evening, and set off from there tomorrow. I don't know any details yet. We'll air-test as soon as I've made out the crew lists: I'm leaving all the gunnery side in your hands. There are nine of us going from here—and we're leading."

There was plenty to do that morning and afternoon. . . . In fact, until we moved down to Stanton Harcourt at about 9 p.m. Guns had to be harmonized, ammunition checked, turrets and guns tested; all the usual routine jobs before an operational trip . . . only even more so.

I suppose a daylight raid is the ambition of most gunners. It is the time when the gunner really comes into his own and really has a chance to prove himself. It is *his chance* . . . and he will be of some real importance and use.

On so many night trips he sees nothing except a dark curtain around him, with probably some stars showing; he will probably see searchlights and flashes of exploding shells, but he is powerless to do anything against these. His job so often is one of complete inactivity: of cold and discomfort, when all he can do is to sit and stare and be ready, ready for something that time and again never happens.

But on a day raid it would be different! The whole crew would rely on him for safety: the safety of the crew and the aeroplane would be, to a great extent, in his hands.

To me a daylight raid was more or less an unknown quantity, and something of a mystery. It was a new experience, and an experience I did not want to miss. I knew quite a

75

lot about night bombing and what to expect: I knew the
sound and feel and even the smell of flak: I had seen hundreds
of searchlights; I had seen storms and ice, bright moonlit
nights, and nights black with clouds: I had seen bright sunsets
and dawns breaking, but I had not been over enemy country
by day. I had my usual bouts of 'stage fright'; my usual qualms,
and that dull feeling in my stomach which with me always
goes hand in glove with any operational trip . . . but, nevertheless, I was glad to be going, glad of a new experience, and
I had a feeling of excitement and almost pleasurable antici-
pation.

As this was to be a day raid and not a routine night trip
we had a picked crew. There were Braddles; Blake, second
pilot; Nick, navigator; Jerry, wireless operator; Wheeler,
engineer; and I chose a Canadian—Berry—as front gunner.
I was in the tail.

Blake was a young sergeant pilot, and a Somersetshire
man. He had been in one or two night raids; but, like the rest
of us, this was his first day raid and he was very thrilled at the
prospect of going. Nick, who had recently been commissioned,
was twenty years of age, and one of the best navigators we
had: he was very keen and really knew his job, and he had
done over forty trips. Jerry was another very experienced
man, and about the same age as Nick: he, too, was very keen,
and seemed to take a real pleasure in everything he did.

I chose Berry because of his keenness to fly. He had not
done an operational trip as yet, but I felt confident that I
could rely on him. He had been with us for about a month,
and was waiting to be crewed up. I think he was very disappointed at not being put on crew sooner. His one ambition
was to fly operationally, and I felt quite happy about having
him in the nose of our aeroplane.

We did our air-test at about eleven o'clock and Braddles
was well satisfied with everything. It was one of those hot July
days with a slight breeze and very clear visibility, and it was a
real pleasure to be flying. The ground below showed clear and
neat, like some intricate patchwork quilt made up of an infinite number of shades and different materials. I thought
also that it looked rather like some gigantic jig-saw puzzle;
each field or wood or village being a piece in the puzzle, and all
fitting perfectly together. It consisted of thousands of pieces,

which did not make a picture, but rather some abstract design and a masterpiece in pattern and colour. The cornfields were ripening and were a lovely golden brown, and newly cut hayfields showed clearly the marks of the mower. On some hayfields the cutting was not finished, and there were square and rectangular shapes in the middle where the grass was still standing. No two fields were the same shape, and very few were the same colour; woods and trees showed in dark patches and dots, and all appeared perfectly flat. There was no indication of any undulation or roughness: all seemed smooth and neat and rather unreal. Roads twisted about as pale thin streaks, and rivers looked like pieces of fine ribbon or threads of silk curling about, yet fitting in perfectly with the pattern. Houses and cottages were like tiny, perfectly made models nestling amongst the trees and woods.

There were some light fleecy clouds between us and the ground which threw dark shadows across the pattern below us. Our own shadow was racing across the ground like a little demon: leaping across hedges and houses and trees alike, sometimes disappearing when it crossed the cloud shadows, and then reappearing again on the other side. The whole scene was fresh and clean and ever-changing, and one at which I could never tire of looking.

There was no sign of discord: the puzzle was complete and no piece was missing. I had very little to do in my turret once I had satisfied myself that everything was as it should be, and soon I gave myself up to the beauty below me; a beauty of ever-changing colours and of calm and peace.

Although we were up there not for pleasure, and not for seeking beauty, but in preparation for our task on the morrow, when we might suffer and probably cause suffering to others ... yet I drove the thought from my mind as something unfit for our present surroundings, and thought only of the present and the far future. The near future—and its final issue—was too uncertain for prolonged thought, while the far future was sufficiently far off and remote to allow of tranquil and pleasurable thoughts. I had been on too many bombing raids and known danger much too close to allow myself to think beforehand of what could and might happen. The thought was ever-present, but by now I could control my feelings to a certain extent and keep thoughts of dangers that I knew about at the back of my mind. Nevertheless, the thoughts were still there, but under control: my motto was 'Sufficient unto the day'.

As we came down, gradually losing height while approaching the aerodrome, the illusion of the unreality of the ground gradually disappeared, and objects began to take their natural forms. Trees began to look like trees, and houses looked as though they were inhabited. Details began to appear, and people could be seen quite clearly.

As we came in to land the ground seemed to rush by more quickly, and one really had an idea of the speed at which one was travelling, despite the fact that it was considerably reduced for landing. We passed over the edge of the aerodrome at about a hundred feet, and from the tail I could see objects rushing by. There were some workmen on there, and I saw them stop and look up. We were losing height all the time, and once over the runway the pilot closed the throttles and we sank down in our forward rush over the concrete below us.

As we touched the ground there was a screaming sound from the tyres on the concrete, and the runway rushed away from the tail faster than I had ever seen any road move before me in a car. The tail wheel was bouncing up and down, and I was being bumped in my turret. We came to a standstill in a remarkably short distance, and turned off to the right to taxi to our parking-place.

The ground crew were waiting for us, anxious for our report on the aeroplane's behaviour. Armourers came to me to ask how the turret behaved. I was well satisfied, and told them so.

Other aircraft were landing from their air-test, and we saw some of them coming in. We watched them for a few minutes, although we could see them landing any day, for there is always something fascinating about seeing a heavy aeroplane land. Some made perfect landings and ran smoothly over the runways once their wheels touched the ground, while others were not so good, and bounced up into the air and down again, and rose several more times until they were going too slowly to leave the ground any more.

Each time an aeroplane landed and the wheels touched the ground a wave of blue smoke was left behind. This was caused by the rubber burning from the sudden friction when the tyres first touched the ground at a speed of about a hundred miles an hour. The wear on those tyres, strong as they are, must be terrific.

During lunch there was no talk of the coming raid, although it was probably the main thought at the back of most of our minds. I know it was with me! We all knew that the success of the raid—and our own lives—depended to a large extent on absolute secrecy and, to a certain extent, on our keeping our mouths shut.

In the afternoon I went out to our aircraft and watched her being bombed-up. It was the first time I had seen any heavy-armour-piercing bombs at close quarters. They were long, evil-looking brutes, thinner than the ordinary bomb, and really looking as though they were capable of enormous damage. To the armourers this was an every-day job, a job requiring considerable skill, but one at which they were expert through constant practice and thorough training. Sometimes when they had finished they would chalk messages on the bombs, such as—'To Hitler from me', or 'Love and kisses to Jerry'—or something similar. Sometimes an aeroplane would not be ready for bombing, for some reason or other, until shortly before take-off time—which might not be until late at night or in the early hours of the morning—yet the armourers would carry out this job as cheerfully and thoroughly as though they had just come on duty, although they would probably have been waiting for hours. Occasionally an aeroplane would not take off at all, owing to trouble at the last moment, and the bomb load would have to be removed. This is a long and tiring business, particularly in the dark, and means collecting the bomb trolleys and winches for lowering the bombs on to the trolleys: it means getting a tractor to tow the trolleys back to the bomb dump . . . and altogether entails probably well over an hour's work . . . yet the only feeling of discontent that I have ever seen the armourers show is that there would be so many less bombs to drop on Germany that night!

The armourers inside our aeroplane were winding the bombs into their racks by means of winches, which sounded like enlarged fishing reels or grandfather clocks being wound. Other armourers below were steadying the bombs and shouting directions to those inside. It seemed to me a complicated business, with much shouting from those outside to those

inside, mingled with many—and by their repetition monotonous—swear words. But the job was completed without a
hitch in a remarkably short time.

As I looked at the bombs lying side by side in their racks,
only waiting for Nick to press the button to release them, I
wondered if they would find their mark. Accurate bombing
from a high level is much more difficult than people realize.

In order to bomb accurately, the aeroplane has to fly
absolutely straight and be quite level during the time the
navigator is sighting his target—which is the 'run-up'—and
until after the bombs have gone. Any slight inaccuracy of
flying, such as a turn off course of even one degree just as the
bomb-aimer is about to release the bombs, might throw them
hundreds of feet off their mark. If the nose of the aeroplane
drops or rises the slightest bit the bombs will fall well short of,
or far beyond, their aiming-point. Often during the run-up
one is being shot at from the ground, and shells burst all around
the aeroplane. Sometimes the bursts are so close that the aircraft is blown many feet by the blast: sometimes she is blown
on her side, and almost out of control, and is made to stall and
fall into a spin or a dive until she can be righted. If any of
these things should happen just as the bomb-aimer is about to
release the bombs, they may fall as much as a mile or more
away from where they were intended to drop.

Even if the opposition is not near enough to be felt, the
bomb-aimer and pilot have to have perfect co-operation and
understanding. The bomb-aimer lies in the nose of the aeroplane, where his bomb sight is set so that he can see the ground
through his sight immediately in front and below him. He will
have to release the bombs well before the aeroplane is over the
target, as they will have the forward motion of the aircraft as
well as their own drop. Bombs of varying shapes and weights
will have their own peculiarities of drop for which allowances
have to be made: the height and speed of the aeroplane at the
time of dropping the bombs have to be set on the sight; also
the direction and velocity of the wind. It can be seen that
bomb-aiming is a very difficult business, and one that requires
a great deal of skill and practice on the part of the bomb-
aimer.

I went round to the tail to have another look at my turret
and guns, and I wondered if I should have to use them.

We arrived at Stanton Harcourt just as it was getting dusk, and had several miles to drive to the Mess, where they had supper ready for us. I saw several people there whom I knew and had not seen for some time, but I did not stay up talking long, as we had to be up early next morning, and had to be fresh. There was not room for us all to sleep in the Mess, so there were beds put ready for us in the Roman Catholic chapel—as it was apparently the only available space they had. We did not know until the following morning that we had been sleeping in a chapel, and I hope we did not desecrate it: had we known I don't know whether we would have been more subdued, as we were in high spirits, and there was considerable horseplay and ragging.

We were wakened next morning at five o'clock. There was a thick white mist which completely obscured objects thirty yards away, and it considerably damped my spirits. Everyone said it was heat mist, and would clear when the sun got stronger . . . but it looked pretty hopeless at the moment, and I thought it might hang about for hours.

Briefing was at seven o'clock, and we were due to take off at ten-thirty. Briefing was less formal than usual, as we were in a make-shift hut so unlike our own briefing-room, with its walls hung with maps and charts and photographs . . . but the Colonel was there and in his usual good form despite the early hour. The Colonel was our intelligence officer. Actually, he had been up all night collecting the latest information and weather reports, and working with the C.O. and Navigation Officer on our route.

The *Scharnhorst* was our target, and she was lying at La Pallice—which is the harbour to La Rochelle, about two hundred and fifty miles south of Brest and in the Bay of Biscay. We were shown photographs of the harbour, which was easily recognizable as there was an island quite close to it. The *Scharnhorst* was lying alongside what looked like a sea wall or large breakwater running some way out to sea.

We had to drop our bombs from fifteen thousand feet, to allow them to have their full power of penetration. The *Scharnhorst* had vast thicknesses of armour-plating on her decks, and an ordinary bomb would have little or no effect: certainly it would not sink it, although it might do a certain amount of superficial damage. It is necessary for an armour-piercing bomb to be dropped from a great height, in order that it may reach its terminal velocity and so have the necessary power behind it to pierce the thickness of armour before exploding.

There are only two ways of sinking a ship as heavily armoured as the *Scharnhorst*: either torpedoes or heavy armour-piercing bombs. She would be very difficult to hit, lying as she was by herself, and would appear very small at fifteen thousand feet: actually she would look about the size of the small lead ships that children have. Her importance to the Germans was pointed out to us by the Colonel, particularly her importance to them in blockading our supplies crossing the Atlantic. It was essential that she should be kept out of commission or sunk. She was a very difficult target, and we had to make every effort to hit her: the raid was timed to take place to coincide with plans made for another attack that same day on the *Gneisnau*, which was still lying at Brest. The Colonel told us all he could about the organization of both raids.

The mist was clearing as we came out after briefing, and we could see the sky a soft blue. The ground was still blurred and indistinct, but the mist was definitely dispersing: it was evidently going to be another very hot day, and I wondered what I should wear. Obviously it would be sweltering in the aeroplane at low level, but probably rather cold when we got to fifteen thousand feet.

I decided to wear my full flying-suit, but with less on underneath. I would rather be too hot than too cold. If you are too cold you can't concentrate, and altogether feel thoroughly miserable; while if you are too hot all you do is to sweat . . . but you can still think. Granted, both extremes are unpleasant, but still I would rather be too hot.

Definitely we should need to concentrate very hard indeed. We did not know for certain how much opposition we should meet, but it would be considerable, and there were sure to be some fighters.

After briefing was over we still had more than two hours to take-off time. I had left my parachute and flying-kit in the aeroplane, so there was no need to cart anything about with me.

Braddles went off with the C.O., and I called together all

the gunners to have a final discussion of plans and make certain everything was as it should be. We were all in good spirits and keyed up for what was to come: we should probably have to do more than just sit this time! Now that we knew more about the target and where it was, we could go more thoroughly into the details of our plans.

There was some coffee and sandwiches for us at nine o'clock, and we stood about in groups in the sunshine as we ate and drank, discussing the job before us. We drifted gradually into groups consisting of our crews.

Blake told us of an aunt of his who lived about fifty miles from La Rochelle: he said that if he had to bail out, he would try to escape there. This seemed an excellent plan, and we begged him not to forget his pals.

It was turning into a glorious morning as we moved out to our aeroplanes. The sun was already hot, and as it shone on the perspex of the turrets and cabins of the aeroplanes they sparkled and gleamed like so many lights twinkling. The fabric and metal of the aircraft were hot to the touch. Yes, it was a perfect day . . . a day to be bathing in the sea or lazing about in the country . . . and it did not seem to fit in at all with bombing and violence. It was a day for peace and laughing and happiness.

Not that we were unhappy! We weren't! At least nobody looked unhappy. We had been selected for an important raid, and an experience that very few people were privileged to have. There would be dangers, yes . . . but so many things really worth doing were dangerous to a certain extent. Motor-car racing is dangerous up to a point; yet it is a good sport, and those taking part in it do not think of the danger part of it . . . at least, not while they are racing. Danger is a thing of the imagination more than of actual fact: in one's mind one can imagine countless things that could and might happen . . . but they very rarely do happen! When danger does come upon one it is usually so sudden, and very often when one is least expecting it, that one has not the time to be frightened.

The racing motorist does not think of what would happen if he burst a tyre at a hundred miles an hour while he is driving, and even if he does, the thought does not stay with him for long. He may think about it beforehand and make plans accordingly, but he only thinks of it as a possible contingency, and one that he must guard against. The thought, if he allows it to stay with him for long, may cause him considerable worry and strain, but this is merely 'stage fright'. If he does actually burst a tyre, he is so occupied as to have no time for fear.

So in the air: it is all the endless things that might happen that scare me and give me that horrible 'sinking feeling', yet when danger has been really close I have usually been too occupied to be frightened.

As I stood by our aeroplane I was excited at the prospect of a new experience, but that numb feeling at the bottom of my chest, and the dryness in my throat, came back as I started to get into my flying-kit. Somehow, dressing in flying clothing seemed to me to be symbolical of dangers and death. As I slowly and methodically dressed I cursed my imagination and myself for being a fool . . . as all the stories I had heard of the more unpleasant side of flying and aerial warfare raced through my mind. I looked at the others, and wondered if they were feeling the same.

Braddles was talking to the C.O. and the Colonel—who was prodding him in the chest with the stem of his pipe and grinning his cherubic grin. Nick and Jerry were smoking cigarettes and joking. Blake was being helped into his 'Mae West' by one of the ground crew. Wheeler was looking up at one of the engines as though he were talking to it, and Berry was standing beside me already fully clothed. They all looked perfectly normal, and I suppose I looked the same. I remember having exactly the same feeling while standing outside the headmaster's study at school waiting for a probable beating. I was not frightened—unless you can call 'stage fright' being frightened —I was more apprehensive. If anyone had come to me and said "May I go instead of you?"—I would have said "No!" without hesitation, even if I had been in the position to say otherwise.

By the time I was fully clothed I was wet through to my tunic with perspiration, and was beginning to think I was a bit of a fool to wear so many clothes, but I consoled myself with the thought that I would probably be glad of them at fifteen thousand feet!

Braddles climbed into the aeroplane, followed by Wheeler and Blake. The C.O. and the Colonel, after wishing us luck, had moved off to say good-bye to the other crews. I intended to wait until the last moment before getting in, as it was cooler outside than in the aeroplane.

I heard one of the ground crew call up to Braddles, who was in his pilot's seat: "Contact port outer." Almost immediately the airscrew blades of the port outer engine began to turn slowly, and then burst into life. It was followed in turn by the port inner engine . . . then the starboard outer . . . and finally the starboard inner engine. I stood behind the engines so as to get the draught from their slipstream: I turned my face towards them with my head lifted, and felt the cool air fanning my skin, and I stood there for several seconds taking deep breaths.

Jerry scrambled in, as excited as a schoolboy at an outing. Nick followed him, with his satchel full of maps, and he was closely followed by Berry. I followed suit.

The heat in my turret was stifling, and the sweat was soon pouring off me. I fastened my helmet as lightly as possible, and plugged in the intercom. Braddles was asking Wheeler about the engine temperatures.

However slow and deliberate Wheeler might appear on the ground, when he was in the air and on the job his reactions always seemed to be instantaneous. He seemed to be anticipating Braddles's question, because he answered immediately. I had noticed the same thing on many other occasions. His replies were always quite definite, too: I have known Braddles say to him—"Are you sure?" and he would always reply— "Quite sure, sir." And he was always right!

No wonder Braddles used to insist on having Wheeler in his crew. He once said to me, *"Riv., old boy, there are two people I insist on having with me, and they are you and Wheeler!"*

As Braddles ran up the engines, clouds of dust were thrown up by the slipstream, completely obscuring my vision. When the engines were running normally again, I signalled to an armourer who was standing near to dust the outside of my perspex for me. As he was finishing rubbing it over we started to move: he walked a few steps with us, still polishing, and then gave a cheery wave of his hand and a grin, and rejoined his pals.

When we moved on to the runway preparatory to take-off, I saw the usual group of people standing watching us set out. The group was larger than usual: I recognized the C.O. and the Colonel, but there were several whom I did not know.

The tail shook and vibrated as the engines roared, and I could feel the aircraft straining, ready to leap forward. The runway raced beneath me faster and faster and appeared to drop away lower and lower . . . and its place was taken by fields below me. I looked back and saw the next aircraft already in position; and that, too, started to move down the runway.

I was feeling perfectly normal now, and quite impersonal, and seemed to be working from outside myself. I was not an individual any longer, but part of a team.

Braddles set course straight away, and we climbed gently. He called through to me and asked me if I could see any of the others . . . and I told him that numbers two and three were airborne, and that I could just see number four on the runway. I spent the next half-hour of the trip reporting to Braddles on the movements of the formation.

Number two was the first to come into position on our right. The pilot's name was Johnny, and I could see him sitting with one hand on the control column and the other on the throttles. He would be tired before the trip was over, as formation flying needs a lot of concentration. The leader is all right, as he simply has to fly on a straight course . . . but those formating on him have to make continual corrections in their flying, as no two aeroplanes can fly exactly alike. No aeroplane can fly absolutely straight and level for long: there are continual atmospheric changes which affect its flight and cause it to drop and rise and turn a degree or two every so often.

Johnny was one of those large, quiet, and absolutely unshakable men: his tail gunner told me that he was always the same, and completely calm no matter what happened. On one occasion when a shell burst particularly close behind the tail and tore a large chunk out of the tail plane, the gunner reported it through to Johnny, who said in a casual way: *"Has it burst yet?"* The gunner replied that it had, whereupon Johnny said: *"You're not dead yet, are you? . . . No. Well, what are you worrying about, then?"* But he said it in such a way as to make the gunner feel quite confident and happy. Most gunners get very attached to their pilots, and I know this one worshipped Johnny. Incidentally, Johnny thought the world of his gunner.

The other aircraft, one by one, came into position. We flew in three separate formations of three aircraft each, with our own aeroplane leading, and one on either side of us and slightly behind. There was another group of three about two hundred yards on our starboard and behind, with another three in a corresponding position on our port.

As I looked at the aircraft behind me I thought they seemed like some impersonal monsters . . . and it was strange to think that they each contained seven men: seven individuals, each with his own life and each capable of deep feeling. We were all bent on the same object: all out to destroy a ship that was a menace to civilization. We would do all in our power to prevent that ship from doing the job for which it was intended.

While I watched the other aeroplanes I wondered how those people would be feeling, and of what they would be thinking. The pilots and navigators, I knew, would be too busy to let their thoughts wander, but the other people would not have much to do yet. The gunners would be sitting in their turrets—as I was—looking about them and probably talking occasionally to their pilots or other members of their crews, and they would be chewing gum or sucking barley sugar. Some, I believe, knew they would not return. One gunner I was told about afterwards, had given full instructions as to what he wanted done with his body. He had his head blown off by a cannon shell! I was talking to him a few minutes before we went to our aeroplanes: he was cheerful and appeared quite unconcerned, and might almost have been setting out on a flight across England only.

I once had the feeling that *I* should not return, and it was like a nightmare that lasted all day. We were detailed for some target in the Ruhr, and as soon as I knew in the morning that we were flying that night I had the most horrible feeling I had ever experienced, which got worse as the day went on. It was far worse than the usual 'stage fright' I always get, and it was with me all day, increasing in intensity. I can't describe what I felt or experienced, as it had no concrete form, but it was a feeling of utter helplessness and depression and was with me in everything I did; it occupied my whole mind, and try as I would, I could not shake it from me.

When we went to do our air-test in the morning there was some trouble with one of the engines, and we had to wait until later. When we eventually got down just before lunch it was found that one of the radiators was leaking, and it had to be changed.

That afternoon I played tennis, hoping to clear my mind by means of some hard exercise, but the depression still persisted, and I found I could not concentrate on the game, try as I would: I would throw up the ball for service, and between throwing it and hitting it my mind would go through torment.

So it went on all through the day, and until I got into my turret that evening. I thought that, maybe, when I got into the aeroplane I should feel all right . . . but no, the feeling was still there.

When the engines were running I tested the illuminated sight. It would not function, although it had been perfectly all right when I had tried it in the morning, so I called through to Braddles to tell him. I tried another bulb, but that would not work either. An armourer was sent speeding for a new part, which was fitted, and the sight was O.K. We started to taxi out to the take-off point, and, on the way, further technical trouble started, so we went back to have it seen to. It was found that it was too long a job to be ready in time, so we were ordered to stay on the ground. We were detailed to fly again two nights later . . . and that time I felt perfectly normal.

The sun was beating down on to my turret, and the sweat was running freely out of me: my face was wet, and my clothes were sticking to my body. The sky was absolutely cloudless; the mist had cleared, and I could see for miles.

I could see every detail of the ground below. We were over country I knew very well, having motored over it many times, and I was thrilled when we passed over landmarks I recognized. Most of these landmarks brought back memories of holidays; of people I was with, or of people I was going to see. I began thinking of those people, and I realized with a shock how many I had lost touch with since the war began. Some, no doubt, were continuing as they always had done, with the routine of their lives altered very little by the war: some, like myself, would be fighting . . . and others I knew had been killed. Some people who were fighting were rather revelling in it, and probably having a jolly sight better time than they did in peace-time; some would be fighting because they had to, and others because they felt they ought to.

I was glad for many of those who were not fighting, and I hoped that they would never have to. Some people are too gentle and ordered in their lives to fight or be concerned in fighting, and I hoped that those people would never see violence or bloodshed. I thought of my old grandmother, who lived through the bombing of London and died after the worst of it was over. I don't think she was ever really frightened, and I think she was proud to know that she was in the war . . . in her beloved London . . . and was holding her own. She once told me that she found the raids *inconvenient*, but said she slept better when the guns were firing. Nothing would induce her to move, even when the flat above her was gutted by a fire bomb. That is the spirit which will never be broken, and the spirit that the Nazis can never understand!

My grandmother loved a fight, and she was always quarrelling with her nurses. On one occasion when she was ill and in bed the nurse who was attending her dropped a tray, whereupon my grandmother quite rightly screamed. The nurse bent over her and said—"Poor old thing!" This infuriated my grandmother so much that she said without a moment's hesitation—"*I may be poor; I grant you I am old . . . but I am not a THING! You are dismissed!*"

We were over the hilly and more broken country of the west counties, and some of the higher hills were only a few hundred feet below us. The rivers, looking invitingly cool, were sparkling in the bright sunlight as they wound about the valleys, sometimes hidden by the woods and trees. I had fished some of these rivers . . . and I tried to see if I could recognize any of the stretches I had actually visited.

We crossed over Dartmoor, with its great expanse of heath and rock and bog. The surface of the hills made them look less ferocious than they really are. I could see the sheep and ponies grazing peacefully in the sunshine, and quite oblivious of our scrutiny. These rugged expanses of hill and rock seemed much less awe-inspiring and more approachable as we sped a few hundred feet above their tops.

I felt I wanted to get out and walk, walk for miles as far as I could see. Those moorland hills seemed to be calling out to me to join them.

The tors looked almost neatly placed on the highest tops of the moors, instead of being great rugged hunks of granite.

Actually, the beauty and charm and magic of those moors
was diminished as their size decreased: viewed from above,
they were gentler, more subdued, less wild than they really are.
The streams were like pale blue threads trickling through the
valleys and down the slopes; the grey stone cottages seemed, if
anything, even more isolated and lonely than they actually
are, as I could see the miles of empty moorland surrounding
them. I had been on Dartmoor and had seen her under all her
variety of moods and changes, but this was the first time that
I had seen her from above. Her beauty from here was quite
new to me: she seemed more gentle and more easy to know,
and I felt I ought to be reintroduced.

I had camped on Dartmoor just over a year before, and it
looked as though we were going to pass very close to our camp
site now: I was getting excited as I recognized parts of the
moor that I knew very well. We were very near the spot where
we had pitched our tent . . . and I was getting more and
more thrilled: I forgot all about the mission that we were on,
and it was like meeting an old friend whom one had not seen
for a long time.

Yes, there was the actual spot where our tent had been
pitched! There was the stream where we had got our water . . .
the old dead tree we had used for firewood . . . the stone wall
over which we had had to climb to reach our tent . . . and
countless other little familiar things that were like friends. I
felt I wanted to get out and renew my acquaintance with
them all: they seemed part of a different life somehow. A lot
had happened to me since then, far more than I had ever
thought would happen, and I would not have missed any of it.
I used to read with envy about the adventures of other people
and wonder if ever I should see any real excitement.

We left Tavistock on our right, and could just see some
ruins in Plymouth on our left. Although the tail gunner sits
with his back towards the direction of travel, if he sees something on his left-hand side, he refers to it as being on the right
or starboard. This saves any form of confusion, and the pilot
knows that if his gunner reports, let us say, a fighter on the
starboard . . . it is on the right-hand side of the *aeroplane,* and
not the gunner's right hand. The sky is divided into areas
around the aeroplane—each area occupying an angle of forty-
five degrees—and they are referred to in naval terms. Thus,

'starboard bow' would be somewhere ahead but on the right
... 'port quarter' would be somewhere behind but on the left
... and 'port or starboard beam' would be on the left- or
right-hand side.

We crossed the coast and flew almost parallel with it for
some distance. The sea was a lovely blue, and very calm. Near
the shore it was extraordinarily clear, and I could see light
patches below the water where there was sand, and dark
patches where there were rocks and seaweed. There were many
people bathing ... and they might have been watching us.
When they read about the raid next day, or heard about it on
the wireless, they would probably remember us and tell their
friends that they had seen a formation of bombers going over.
If they guessed we were on a raid when we passed over, perhaps
they would wish us luck.

As we moved farther away from the coast I could no longer
see any people. I missed those people bathing and walking
along the beaches: although they were all strangers and
probably I should never seen them again, yet they were part
of England. England that was getting farther away and that
would soon be out of sight. I felt slightly homesick as the
coastline got thinner and less distinct.

I called through to Braddles and told him that I was going
to test my guns, and he told me to carry on. I pointed the guns
downward and pressed the firing button.

There was slight vibration as the guns fired, and a few
seconds later I could see splashes in the sea as the bullets hit
the water. I felt comforted at this power in front of me. If I
should have to use it I would have to be cool and think quickly
... but I had the necessary power, and the knowledge to use it,
and the rest was up to me.

I heard Berry ask if he should test his guns, and shortly
afterwards I heard him say—"My guns are O.K., Captain!"

CHAPTER VII

OUR shadows sped across the sea below, keeping us company all the way. We were flying south, and I called through to Berry and told him to keep a careful look-out and to beware of attacks from out of the sun. A fighter will very often attack from the glare of the sun, if he can, and it is very necessary to keep a close watch in that direction.

When we reached the Bay of Biscay there were a lot of small fishing-boats about. Some looked like steam trawlers, while others had sails, some of which were brightly coloured. They were a lovely sight in the bright sunshine, with their colours standing out vividly against the blue background of the sea. I wondered if they were French or German, but whichever they were, they looked very picturesque and peaceful. They were probably wondering far more . . . who we were and where we were going! I hoped none of them were carrying wireless transmission sets.

Just as we entered the Bay we saw an open boat crammed with men, obviously a shipwrecked crew. They waved frantically to us as we passed over the top of them, but there was nothing we could do then except note their position: on no account could we use our wireless and risk giving our own position away, thereby jeopardizing our chances of reaching our objective undetected. My heart went out to those men, as I knew to a certain extent what they must be suffering. They must have been overjoyed when they saw us approaching, and felt that surely they would get some help, and their dismay must have been awful when they saw us pass by without apparently noticing them. I wondered how long they had been in that boat, and how much water they had left. They might have been there for days or even weeks. I have often thought about them since, and wondered if they were ever picked up: they were about fifty miles from the coast, and there was no sign of any other shipping near them at the time. I had no idea of their nationality, but I imagined them to be British.

As we climbed, the French coast could just be seen away out on our port side. Occasionally it would disappear as the coastline withdrew into bays. I thought how different that stretch of coast must be to what it was a few years before. It was no longer the playground of the rich and the holiday-makers, but the hiding-place of fighters which might come at us at any moment!

The coast and the sky above us had to be watched very carefully by us, as the direction from which we might expect to be attacked. We were having to be very alert now, as we were well within the range of enemy fighters, and I could no longer afford to let my mind wander, allowing thoughts to drift idly through my mind. My job now was to defend our aeroplane: I was its ears . . . and, if necessary, its *sting*! My job was just beginning. I could afford to be idle up to now, but now I must be on the watch: I must concentrate . . . alert and ready . . . ready for instant action. At any moment a fighter might dive down at us out of the sun, undetected by those in front.

I could sense the tension throughout the whole crew. No longer was there any idle chatter, remarking on things we had seen, or things of little importance, but a silence to be broken only by a remark vital to the job in hand. Each man was look-ing, searching intently in the direction most convenient to his position in the aeroplane.

The silence was broken by Nick exclaiming—"I can see a ship ahead. She looks like a cruiser!"

Braddles swore. It would mean that as soon as we were spotted, our position, course, and even height would be signalled all along the coast—even if it had not been done already by one of the trawlers over which we had passed! Our alertness and the concentration in our search was, if anything, intensified when we heard Nick's report.

Within a few minutes the ship opened fire on us, and I saw puffs of smoke appear in amongst the formation as if from nowhere. I immediately called through to Braddles to tell him, but almost before I had finished speaking there was a salvo right underneath! We could hear the shells bursting with their dull thuds very close to us, and at the same time the aeroplane would lurch as it was buffeted by the blast. They had got our range and height accurately straight away, and for the next few minutes we had to fly through the barrage around us.

The sky was getting thick with the smoke from bursting

shells, and several times I could smell the acrid stink of burnt explosives as we flew through the fumes. More shells were bursting all the time, and I could see their yellow flashes followed instantly by grey puffs as they spread themselves across the sky. Sometimes they would burst just beside or underneath the aeroplane, which would heel over or appear to jump up several feet; sometimes there would be a string of grey puffs just beside us, dark at first, but getting lighter, which would rush by and be broken up as Johnny or some other aeroplane flew through them . . . or sometimes they would continue rushing past just above or below the aeroplanes, and be joined by more of the devilish little clouds. Occasionally I actually saw the shell on its upward flight, looking like a silver streak soaring upwards, which would suddenly stop and give place to a grey puff. It was never alone; always surrounded and followed by others. Those near us could be heard and felt and sometimes even smelt; the muffled thud of the explosions was rather like the noise a brick might make as it hits the water when dropped down a deep well.

Nobody spoke. We were too intent controlling our emotions. I sat perfectly still in my turret, watching—fascinated—this fury about me and wishing it would stop! It was too close for my comfort and peace of mind; it only needed a shell to burst a few feet nearer to us than those were doing already, and we should be blown from the sky.

When we passed over the ship I was able to see her. How small she looked—just like a toy—to be sending up so many shells! It seemed strange to think that there were men—our enemies—below, working furiously in the hot sunshine to fire and reload the guns. Probably they would be cursing the sudden intrusion, and wondering what it was all about.

The ship was taking no chances, either. Obviously she thought she might be our target . . . for she was zig-zagging about all over the surface of the water. She was safe, however, as we were after bigger fry!

When we got out of range of her guns the barrage ceased, and we continued on our way as before. No one had been shot down or seriously damaged, as far as I could see.

We were still in formation, and were flying as though nothing untoward had happened. The sky was absolutely clear except for a grey haze behind us where the smoke from the shells still lingered as a reminder of the interruption a few moments before. The ship had finished her snaking and had settled down to a straight course, as I could see from the wake she left behind her.

"Another fifteen minutes'll see us there," said Nick down the intercom.

"Keep a very careful look-out, everybody!" said Braddles.

We were nearer the French coast now, and I could just distinguish the fields and woods. I should have liked to be able to look longer at the coast, as this was the first time I had flown near France in the daytime, but I had to search the sky above, below, and all around me. My eyes ached, staring and straining into the dazzling blue of the sky. If there were fighters about we should soon see them, as we were very near our destination.

Berry suddenly said one word—"Fighters!"—down the intercom.

Whether he intended the effect to be dramatic I don't know: probably not. Nevertheless, the word sounded distinctly dramatic, coming as it did through the intercom. in his Canadian accent after a silence of ten minutes, and it was followed a few seconds later by—"They're away out on our port beam!"

They were too far round for me to see them . . . but in a few seconds I saw three more, flying in formation several miles away and well above us. They were not closing in, but were flying from the port quarter round to the starboard quarter, and I gave their position and range to Braddles.

"There are some more climbing up," Berry said.

Evidently they did not intend to attack until they were up in full force: they seemed to be sizing us up, and wondering how formidable a target we should be. Well . . . they were soon to find out!

More fighters were still climbing up to join those already up there. I could see three formations of three, which were shortly joined by six more. They were all about three miles away, and showed no signs of coming in yet. Berry said he could see about twelve more from the nose which were flying across our track and all several miles away.

Still they did not come in to attack. Evidently they did not consider themselves strong enough even yet.

Johnny had closed right in to us with his wing tip only a

few feet from our tail; and it was the same with number three. They came close in for mutual support, as the nearer they flew to us the better we should be able to protect ourselves by the combined fire from our turrets. Braddles was flying very well, and the others were able to formate perfectly.

Any hope we had had of carrying out a surprise attack had been forestalled, probably by the cruiser we had flown over a quarter of an hour before. They were waiting for us with their fighters and their guns, and we should have to fight our way in and out again. More fighters were in the sky, and still they seemed content to wait.

We were within a few minutes of the target, and Nick said he could see it clearly. The rest of the formation got into position ready to drop their bombs.

I sat keyed up and waiting, waiting for what should come. Sitting waiting to be attacked was a great strain. When were they going to come at us? We continued on, ever nearer the target, and the fighters flew around us about two miles away. I waited . . . ready. . . .

Suddenly the tell-tale puffs of smoke appeared! There were dozens of them and all around us, and as we moved, fresh ones followed us. I was not watching out for the shell bursts, though I could see them and feel them and hear them all the time: I was looking around for fighters, watching those I could see, and searching the sky for fresh ones. . . .

The sky behind us was getting thick with the fumes and smoke of shell bursts. They were firing all they had got right at us, and as hard as they could. The thirty guns from the *Scharnhorst* were blazing away, supported by many more from the shore.

The crump of the shells around and below us was incessant, and many times I was blown hard against the side of my turret or off the seat . . . yet I hardly noticed the barrage: I was waiting, waiting to be attacked, waiting to defend our aeroplane from the fighters that were ever increasing in numbers and were flying around us and above us, yet had not as yet started their assault.

The sky was getting very thick with smoke, and it was difficult to see. I no longer had a clear, unobstructed view around me: it was rather like looking through a fog or a thick haze, with fresh clouds appearing continuously.

With black smoke pouring from the engines

Jerry and Blake had gone back into the fuselage to man the beam guns, which were situated two on either side and about half-way along the fuselage. They were standing there looking out and waiting for attacks.

Suddenly the fighters seemed to be amongst us! . . . diving, climbing and twisting amongst us! For the moment our aeroplane was left alone, and those behind us were getting the brunt of the attacks.

The fighters were in amongst the flak bursts, which died down considerably when they started their attacks. I saw one burst into flames, roll over on its back, and dive down towards the sea, leaving a trail of black smoke behind it. Almost at the same time I saw one of our own aeroplanes diving down with smoke pouring from two of its engines, and with three fighters on its tail. I could not tell which one it was or who was in it, and I did not dare to watch it for long as I could not keep my eyes fixed in one place for more than a few seconds: I was continually looking around me, turning my turret first one way and then the other, and peering through the clouds . . . now in parts looking like storm clouds and all the time increasing.

All the time Johnny was near us, following our every move. I saw two fighters diving on his tail from above . . . one of them continued on its dive past his tail with smoke belching from it!

Through all the medley and the noise of shell bursts around us I heard Nick giving direction to Braddles in his bombing run-up: he sounded entirely oblivious to the hell let loose around him, and only conscious of the target below him. As I heard him giving his directions of 'lefts', 'rights', and 'steadys', I could feel the aeroplane turn and check as Braddles made the corrections. "*Bombs gone!*" he finally said; then, almost immediately, "I got a *wizard* sight."

All the time I was waiting and wondering why we were not being attacked: I almost wished we were, as I could do something then. As it was, all I could do was to sit and watch, and wait . . . wait for our turn and watch our aeroplanes being shot at!

Under normal conditions I should have been absorbed and scared by the flak bursting so frequently and so near us. The crumps underneath, behind, and on either side of us seemed to follow one another almost without pause. Several times I felt the jar and thud as splinters hit us and tore through the fuselage and tail . . . yet only part of my mind registered and realized the fact. I could do nothing about it, anyway. I could only sit and watch and hope that we should get no fatal hits. My mind was absorbed with the fighters, and wondering when they were going to attack. I *could* do something with them . . . that was what I was there for. I was there to fight back, but I could not fight unless they first came at us. That was what was getting me down; watching them, waiting, and unable to do anything.

Almost as soon as Nick said—*"Bombs gone!"*—I saw a fighter diving down on us. I immediately called through to Braddles:

"Fighter diving down port quarter up!"

I started giving him directions for turning, and at the same time I elevated my guns to meet the attack. As we turned, the fighter passed over the top of us, and disappeared from my range of vision.

As soon as I lost sight of this one, I saw another one climbing up at us, and again I called through to Braddles:

"Fighter starboard quarter down!"

The fighter started firing at us almost as soon as I spotted it, and I saw the flashes from his guns and the tracers streaking past us. He was using cannon, and was really out of range of my machine-guns. However, I opened fire, hoping to put him off, as I had plenty of ammunition and could afford to use it. He came steadily in, firing in bursts, and I replied with my guns: he still came in, getting nearer . . . and still I fired back. I could hear and feel his shells and bullets striking the fuselage just behind me, and still he came in, ever nearer. I felt no antagonism, but was calm yet determined to shoot him down.

I felt as a boxer or a duellist might feel, pitting his skill against that of his opponent. 'Why hasn't he gone down?' I kept thinking. . . .'Surely I must be hitting him?'—yet he was still able to hit back, and his tracers still kept streaming past me! 'And why haven't I been hit?' I thought, as he still kept closing in. We were twisting about the sky and he was following us, shooting all the time.

I had no feeling of fright, only of amazement that I had not shot him down, as we seemed to have been shooting at each other for so long. I was also amazed that I had not been hit, as the bullets and cannon shells were pouring all around me continuously. Perhaps I had been hit and did not know it; I would look around afterwards.

Out of the corner of my eye I saw part of the tail plane ripped away by a cannon shell, and almost at the same time the fighter rolled over on his back and went into a spin! I felt a vast feeling of relief surge through me as I called through to Braddles and said: "I've got him!"

The whole combat seemed to have gone on for a very long time, although really it could have lasted only for a few seconds. I began to feel very scared. I was too intent while we were being attacked, to feel at all frightened, but now that there was a lull from activity against us for a few seconds, I felt my heart pounding against my chest, and my throat and mouth felt dry. Outwardly I was perfectly calm, though, and ready for further attacks.

Almost as soon as I said—"I've got him"—I heard Blake calling:

"Jerry has been hit, sir."

"Is he bad?" Braddles asked.

"Yes, sir. I think so. I'm doing all I can."

All around us the shells were bursting and the air was even blacker with smoke now, like great dark clouds through which we were flying. Bombers and fighters were flying and twisting amongst it. I saw another Halifax diving down with smoke pouring from it, and two more fighters diving to their doom, one in flames and the other obviously out of control. I could see another Halifax with three fighters close behind its tail.

My turret was thick with cordite fumes, which were making me cough.

"I think he's dead, sir," Blake said.

Fighters were all around now, but none were actually attacking us. We were getting away from the flak, and the air was becoming clearer. Two fighters were chasing us from behind, but they were not firing at us yet, and were not within range.

"Where is he hit?" Braddles asked.

"In the chest," Blake answered. "I can't see any other marks."

Jerry was standing by his guns watching out for fighters when he was hit. He was jumping up and down in his excitement, as he had just seen a fighter crash into the sea in flames. Suddenly he turned round and looked at Blake with a surprised expression on his face and slowly sank down and rolled over . . . dead.

The fighters who were chasing us gave up, and I saw them turn away: they had probably had enough for one day, and did not want to get taken too far from their base. Two of my guns had jammed and were out of action: I had noticed they had stopped, as soon as I had ceased firing, but I had decided not to touch them while there was a chance of being attacked again at any moment, but to wait until I had more breathing space. I still had two more guns working, and I felt confident of them in an emergency.

Now that there were no fighters within about half a mile of me, I had a look at the stopped guns. One I was able to put right quite easily, and I fired a short burst to make certain that it was working, but the other one I should have to dismantle when we were well clear of the target.

Johnny was fairly close behind us and on our starboard, with another Halifax slightly behind him, but those were all I could see at the moment. The second one I noticed had white smoke belching from behind one of his engines, which meant that one of his radiators had gone and that very soon that engine would stop. However, he could carry on with three engines quite well.

The area we had just left was thick with what looked like dark, ugly clouds, clouds consisting of smoke fumes hanging like a pall over the target, where twenty minutes before there had been bright blue sky. It seemed to be hanging there in mourning for the dead.

As I watched this dark and dreary mass behind us I saw two more Halifaxes appear: we were making for sea level—or, rather, about a thousand feet above it—and they were doing the same.

"How many Halifaxes can you see from the tail?" Braddles asked.

"I can see three altogether . . . *our* number two, and two others some way behind," I replied.

"Let me know if you see any more."

We were still within sight of the French coast, and I kept a lookout chiefly in that direction.

"How are *you* feeling, Front Gunner?" I asked.

"I'm feeling fine, sir. How about you?"

"I'm O.K.," I replied.

"I'm going to fly well clear of the coast, Navigator," I heard Braddles say to Nick.

I looked round at the tail plane that had been hit: there was a large ragged hole there, and the fabric where it had been ripped away was flapping behind like streamers. I saw that the hole was in the starboard elevator, and that the whole structure was badly damaged.

I called through to Braddles to tell him about it, and he sent Wheeler back to have a look. Wheeler reported that it was O.K., and he also said that the fuselage round by the tail was full of holes. I knew it must be so, as I had heard and felt the bullets and cannon shells hitting and tearing into it. Braddles asked him how the engines were, and he replied that one was running very hot, and that it would probably pack up pretty soon. He also said that one of the tanks must be badly damaged, as it was nearly empty.

We had a good two hours' flying before reaching our own coast, so our position did not look too good. What further damage had been done we could not tell . . . but we were still flying, which was the main thing, anyway.

I felt very depressed. All the excitement I had felt while I was in combat had died down, and reaction had set in. Jerry was lying dead just behind me, and I was thinking of him all the time: I remembered how cheerful and happy and how much alive he had always seemed, and how he had always been smiling and laughing. Less than half an hour ago he had been alive . . . not thinking of himself; only that our trip should be a success . . . and now he was dead; killed by a fighter he never even saw. I had shot down the fighter that killed Jerry, but too late . . . not before Jerry had been killed.

I turned and looked through the glass panel behind my back, and saw him lying on the floor with his helmet still on and his oxygen mask over his face. Blake had folded his hands across his chest. I remembered how I had seen him before, how he had sprung into the aeroplane laughing and so full of life and spirit, and I felt very miserable as I saw him lying there dead and so still. I thought of his mother, and how she would feel: it is those who are left behind who have to suffer.

Blake was sitting beside Jerry with his head between his hands, and he looked about all in, poor chap. I suggested to Braddles that he might go forward now, as we were well away from the target, so he called him.

Blake said he thought he had something in his eye. Actually, there was a tiny shell splinter embedded there! We discovered later that he had three other wounds as well . . . two bullet wounds in his leg and a shell splinter in his shoulder . . . but he said he knew nothing about them and did not even know he had been hit until after he had got out of the aeroplane. He said his leg felt a bit stiff!

We were silent for some time. Reaction from our activity had set in, and I think we all felt rather miserable.

The silence was broken by Berry's Canadian accent:

"Say, Captain, is there a lavatory aboard this ship?"

The tension was broken for me then, as I saw the unconscious humour of his remark, and I was able to laugh, particularly when Braddles said that he had not heard, and asked him to repeat it.

We had lost sight of the French coast, and were flying about a thousand feet above the sea, calm and blue and a vast contrast to the grimness we had left behind. The sun was beating into my turret, and once again I was conscious of the heat.

I felt suffocated in my turret, which still stank with the burnt cordite fumes, and I would have given anything to be able to stand in a cool breeze. I felt very cramped, too, and would have loved to get out and stretch. However, I would have to stay where I was, as it was not safe to leave my turret even for a minute: at any moment more fighters might come at us from the shore, only just beyond the horizon on our starboard. Reports would have been sent all along the coast that we were returning, and even now fighters were probably looking for us. We would not be safe until we reached the shelter of our own shore, still about an hour and a half away.

There were not so many ships and boats about now, as we were considerably farther out to sea than we had been on our outward journey. Those we did see seemed to have lost much of the beauty they had had before.

"D'you know where we are, Navigator?" Braddles asked Nick.

"Not exactly, sir, but I think we're all right. I can't be certain, though, without the wireless."

"How are we off for petrol, Wheeler?"

"About another hour and a half, sir."

"We'll make for the Cornish coast," Braddles decided. "And I'll land at St. Eval!"

This bucked me up quite a lot, as it was quite near my home, and with any luck I should be able to get there that night. I felt I wanted to go home . . . but we were still a long way away. I was very tired.

Johnny was flying in close formation to us again: he had all his four engines running, and I could not see any sign of damage to his machine. Once he flew right over the top of us, and I imagine he was having a close look to see how much damage we had sustained.

The other aircraft had dropped back, about a mile behind. I told Braddles this, and he asked me to let him know if it dropped back any farther. Johnny was evidently worrying about him, too, as he turned around and flew alongside. I reported this to Braddles, who said we would continue on as we were, as Johnny seemed to be O.K.: we would have only just enough petrol to get back as it was, and he could not afford to lose any distance by turning round. Johnny and the other aeroplane were flying together, and there was nothing we could do by flying with them . . . so we continued on alone.

I watched our shadow on the water . . . now all alone . . . and I missed seeing Johnny just behind us: he had seemed so secure and steady. I could still see him and the other aircraft behind us, but they were gradually losing distance.

We were running into some low, misty cloud, which in a way was an advantage, as it would shield us from possible fighter attacks. It looked like a sea mist or fog, and seemed to be right down on the water. When we ran into it I lost sight of the aeroplanes behind us.

The mist was in patches, and we kept flying through it and into bright sunshine again alternately. When we came out of it I could see a film of moisture on the tail plane and on the perspex round my turret. It was quite a relief flying through this mist, as the sun for a short time ceased to blaze down on me, and I felt almost cool.

This misty cloud did not last for long, and once again we flew into clear, cloudless sky. The sun beating down on to the sea below and behind us sent up a dazzling, shimmering brightness which burnt my eyes. I looked at my watch and saw that we had about another forty-five minutes to go before reaching our coast.

Nick gave Braddles a change of course, which meant that we must have been at a point somewhere west of Brest, and were making a turn to starboard to bring us to the Cornish coast. After we turned, the sun was no longer right behind us —which I found a relief—but slightly on our starboard.

There was no sign of shipping or land, only a vast expanse of sea below us, calm and clear and blue, disappearing into a misty horizon. It would be the same sea beating against the shores of Cornwall, a coast I knew and loved well.

Unpleasant and uncomfortable thoughts began passing through my mind. I imagined what would happen if Nick was wrong in his navigation . . . if the course he had given Braddles would not take us to the Cornish coast, but past Land's End and up the Irish Sea. We might pass right clear of the west coast and run out of petrol without ever seeing land! Or Wheeler might be wrong in his calculations of our petrol supply, and we might have even less than he thought and run out just as land came in sight! Or the petrol gauges might be wrong, and even at this moment the tanks might be nearly dry and the engines sucking their last few gallons.

I drove these thoughts from my mind as being unnecessarily foolish and weak. Nevertheless, they were unpleasant while they lasted.

"How is the petrol, Wheeler?" Braddles asked.

"About another forty-five minutes, sir," Wheeler told him.

"What is our E.T.A. at the coast, Navigator?" Braddles asked again.

"Another thirty minutes should see us there," Nick answered.

"As soon as we hit the coast, give me a course for St. Eval," Braddles said.

We certainly had not much petrol to spare. The aircraft was flying quite steadily, and the engine that Wheeler had his doubts about was still functioning, though it was losing a lot of power.

"I think I can see some land," I heard Berry say from the nose, some time later.

'Pray God he's right!' I thought, and began to feel more cheerful. With land in sight we should soon be back, and an unpleasant day would be just another memory.

There was no sign of the other aircraft: I had not seen anything of them since we got into the misty clouds. I hoped they were all right. They had probably changed course before we had: one of them was sure to have wireless, in which case they would know exactly where they were.

I peered on either side of me, looking for the land, but I could not see far enough forward. It must have been quite close, as I heard Braddles say to Nick—"Can you get a pin-point yet, Navigator?"

We must have been a bit too far west, for in a moment I heard Nick give a course bringing us farther east.

At last, by leaning forward, I was just able to see the coast some miles away on my right. What a glorious sight it was! I thought that I had never been so pleased to see the shore. It was even better than when returning home at night, as I was able to see it showing clearly in detail in the sunlight, whereas at night usually all one can see is a thin, pale streak.

Our journey was nearly over, and I was just beginning to realize how tired and exhausted I really was. The past few hours had been a great strain owing to the need for constant concentration, and also that uncertainty all the time of wondering if we should make it.

As we crossed the coast, and I was able to look down into the rocks and wonderfully clear sea below, a wave of happiness and relief surged over me. This was *home* . . . and looking at its best, alive and clear and clean. We passed the rocky coast, and over the short green turf and scrubby trees above the cliffs. The cattle and sheep were grazing as I had seen them six hours earlier. We crossed the valleys with their rocky streams . . . the hills criss-crossed with their stone walls . . . over the woods and the little villages all so quiet and peaceful and un-hurried. This was home and England . . . a sight one has to lose and be away from to fully appreciate and enjoy.

The ambulance came alongside after we landed, and I stayed in my turret until Jerry had been lifted from the aeroplane. I had seen him jump in so cheerfully and happily, and I felt I could not bear to see him carried out dead.

There was a group of people round our plane as we got out, and one of them said to me—"Who was he? The tail gunner?"

"No," I replied. "I'm the tail gunner."

We were not the only Halifax to land there; there were four of us altogether. We had parked next to one, and I saw that the tail turret had been nearly blown away. Medical orderlies were still trying to extricate the gunner.

I felt very weak, and sat down on the grass. Someone offered me a cigarette. I said I would smoke my pipe.

.   .   .   .   .

After we had been interrogated and had had a meal and some drinks, I hired a car and drove home, taking Nick with me.

CHAPTER VIII

WHEN I got back to my unit, the first person I saw was Leonard, dressed in his roll-top jersey, just getting ready to set off for Berlin.

"Congratulations, Revs!" he said.

"What for, Leonard?"

"For shooting down a fighter."

"Well, it was either him or us. Who've you got in the tail?"

"Martin."

"Oh, he's all right, but I wish I was coming with you."

"Next time, Revs."

The next time was not Berlin; it was Dusseldorf, but the one after that was Berlin, and I was with him.

I was glad he was taking Martin, chiefly for Martin's sake. He had not flown for some time. The last trip he was on he was wounded by a cannon shell, which exploded in his turret. They were being attacked by a fighter, and the shell that wounded Martin badly damaged his turret, making it very difficult to operate. However, he managed to work it somehow, and shot the fighter down. While he was in hospital his pilot was posted, and I knew that Martin was not happy about flying with just anybody: I felt that Leonard would give him the fresh confidence which he badly needed.

That trip I did to Berlin with Leonard was one of the best I have ever done. Everything was perfect. The moon was full, and we were able to map-read our way across Germany.

I had never seen the ground so distinctly at night before. Fields, rivers, lakes, railways, roads, all showed almost like day: I was even able to distinguish cornfields. The suburbs around Berlin appeared, getting gradually thicker until we were over the city itself. We cruised around—almost like a 'Cook's tour'—and I could see the houses, streets and parks as clearly as though I was looking at an aerial photograph. The moon was so bright that the searchlights were almost ineffective in their attempts to compete with its brilliance.

The guns left us alone that night, too. Whether the shells

were not bursting at our height, or whether we were just lucky, I don't know: anyway, we got off scot free. After we had dropped our bombs we cruised around a bit more before turning north on our long journey home!

.　　.　　.　　.　　.

About this time we had a new C.O., who was known to most people as 'Robby'. He was happiest when he was in the air, and he did not waste time getting there, either! I flew with him on his first trip with the squadron.

As I entered the briefing-room, which was rapidly filling up with air crews, I looked at the map eagerly with the others to see where our target was. Our route was marked by a piece of red tape which terminated at Cologne.

Cologne! I suddenly felt empty inside, and weak. What would happen this time? But perhaps the third time would be lucky. . . .

.　　.　　.　　.　　.

It was a pitch dark night as we circled, dropping flares, searching for our target. The flares showed fields, but that was about all! We were one of the first due over the target, so there would be no fires to guide us.

There *were* fires, though, but most of them were very obviously dummies. They were too even and without smoke . . . or else they were not bright enough . . . or perhaps too bright. A genuine fire looks very red from the air, and sends a glow all around. It is not a consistent mass of red, either, but it flickers and changes colour . . . and there is *always* smoke.

We continued searching for some time. Both Robby and the navigator were convinced we were near Cologne . . . but there were no searchlights, no flak . . . no one else's flares. We must be early, or else the navigation must be wrong.

Suddenly Cologne awoke, and showed herself some distance away on our port. Her hundreds of guns and searchlights all got busy together. There must have been several aeroplanes over there, too . . . as flares, like yellow balls, were mingled with the flak and the searchlights. They seemed very unconcerned and aloof from the hubbub around them as they floated proudly and majestically down.

"My God! Some poor blighter is getting it," said Robby.

I was watching. About a hundred searchlights were all pointing at one spot, and this point where the beams intersected was alive with sparkles and flashes. It was iridescent and writhing with brilliance as a piece of bad meat moves with maggots. Robby was right: some poor blighter *was* getting it, and getting it badly. Every gun and searchlight in Cologne seemed to be concentrated at that spot, at that aeroplane waiting to drop its bombs.

A red glow appeared amongst the flashes. It divided into two glowing patches which were falling, still held relentlessly by the searchlights. One of the glowing masses exploded, and disintegrated into many more glowing pieces! Still the searchlights followed the burning, wreckage, followed it until the beams were flat with the ground, while flares hovered around, and bombs flashed below.

"*Whew!*" I heard Robby exclaim.

We were over Cologne, searching for our target! Searchlights were making it difficult to see: there were so many of them, and their beams threw a protecting screen of light across the city. They were weaving about the sky looking for another victim: they seemed uncertain as they groped cautiously about the darkness with their long tentacles. Who should it be? Who would they choose? They seemed to be gloating over their last victim and prolonging the impending moment of their next feast.

They decided . . . and were moving in our direction! Some hurried as though eager to be there first, others lingered as though not quite certain, or else prolonging the delicious moment. They came on us singly . . . in pairs . . . and then in dozens.

With them came the flak, bursting everywhere and without pause. Shells above us . . . shells below us . . . shells behind us and on either side. Their noise was deafening, and drowned the roar from the engines. They stayed with us without effort as we turned and twisted, trying to free ourselves from their villainous grasp.

The searchlights dazzled and mocked us as they clawed and pawed with their evil clutches about our aeroplane, trying to snatch it from the sky. The guns were getting angry with them . . . and with each other . . . and with us . . . in their vain attempt at our destruction.

The searchlights were smug and conceited as they fondled us in their filthy fingers. They were holding us steady for the shells to hit . . . but the shells were not hitting hard enough! They must come closer. Look . . . the searchlights were touching us . . . *holding us* . . . holding us tightly in their death grasp! They must come closer . . . must tear right through as they did to their last victim. Think of him . . . how he had gone down burning, with the bodies inside struggling to free themselves!

I was completely blinded in my turret. Everywhere there was light . . . shafts of white and violet light . . . relentlessly rude and inquiring. The light was around my turret . . . taunting me . . . *infuriating* me: I felt I was exposed to hundreds of inquiring cool and piercing eyes!

A shell splinter crashed, tearing through my turret, ripping a great hole in the side. I seemed to be filling all the turret, and I wondered how it missed me. I wished I was smaller and could hide. I felt so exposed and visible, sitting stuck out at the back of the aeroplane surrounded by perspex.

Robby was singing and letting out periodical whoops and war cries. Suddenly he said—"I've got it! I'm going right over it. Get ready, Navigator."

About a minute later he called through to me:

"Could you see them burst, Tail Gunner?"

I had not seen a thing . . . only light.

We had done our job, and were free to leave. The searchlights left us as they had come on to us . . . singly and in numbers. We were clear at last, and flew once more through the darkness . . . which seemed even darker than before. The searchlights were still busy, but not with us . . . they had found another victim, and were tormenting him.

As I watched them getting fainter, a fresh batch shot up from below. There was no indecision about this batch: they were on us straight away with a determined, vice-like grip. They were unaccompanied by flak with an obvious reason . . . *fighters!*

There were as many searchlights as before, and as bright. All I could see was brightness and reflections on the perspex. Was there a fighter behind us? Was he stalking us . . . getting nearer and nearer . . . waiting his chance to let fly? I strained into the dazzling, bright light, turning my turret this way and that.

Suddenly it came! I heard his guns first, and saw red tracer bullets coming at me. As I heard his guns I opened fire, shooting at the flashes that were all I could see of him. I don't know what happened. I only know that as I fired, he stopped firing. It all happened in about three seconds.

"Are you all right, Tail Gunner?"

Robby had seen the tracer shooting past us, and he imagined I had been hit, as I was silent. In my excitement I had forgotten to switch on my intercom.

·　　　·　　　·　　　·　　　·

As we crossed our coast it was getting light, and I was discussing with the navigator the prospects of the wild fowling on the marshes below.

"Stop talking all that rot! We've had enough shooting for today!" Robby interrupted.

CHAPTER IX

ONE morning early in December I was in Leonard's office for my usual morning visit, and the first thing he said to me was—"I've got news for you, Revs."

"What is it? Don't tell me you're posted."

"No, nothing like that. There's to be another *daylight* in the near future."

"Are you flying?" I asked him quickly. "If so, I'm coming with you."

"I'm afraid not, Revs. At least, that's the verdict at the moment. I shall try and work it, though. The Wing Commander is flying, and wants you with him."

"I wish to goodness you were going, Leonard!"

"So do I, Revs, but there we are."

"As you say . . . 'there we are'! D'you know where we're going?"

Leonard pointed to the map and put his finger on Brest.

"But for God's sake, not a word," he added. "Only the Wing Commander, you and I, know the target . . . and it *must* be kept dark."

.   .   .   .   .

I went up to see the Commanding Officer.

"Leonard has told me the news, sir," I said to him.

"I don't know much more than you do yet, Riv," he replied, "but we've got to get in bags of training. Who shall we take as front gunner?"

"I don't know, sir. I'll think it over and let you know."

"We've got to keep this show as quiet as we can," the Wing Commander went on. "I propose to have a meeting of all the flying crews this morning and tell them all I can, but it is essential there is no talking about it afterwards. We've got about another nine days, and we'll spend all the time in formation flying and practice bombing!"

.   .   .   .   .

The weather was good—cold and clear with the ground frozen hard—and we got busy right away. There were to be forty bombers on the job altogether, and we were supplying six of them, with Robby leading. During the days before the actual raid we practised every day: we practised flying in formation and bombing in formation, and we got really good.

I thought it might be a good scheme for the rear gunners to fly with the main perspex panel taken out of their turrets . . . and I took the panel out of mine to try the idea. The first time I tested it we did not go above two thousand feet, and I was delighted with the scheme. It meant that we should have a perfectly clear view behind, as there was nothing to obstruct our vision, the entire front of the turret being exposed to the outside air. But the next time I flew in the open turret we were at fifteen thousand feet, and a temperature of —30 *degrees Centigrade*! Although we were only up at that height for an hour, I thought I had got frostbite. The cold beating in was agonizing, and I felt thoroughly miserable and decided then and there that we should *not* fly with the turrets open!

I enjoyed those days of training and practice. The weather was perfect, and every day was brilliantly clear. We usually flew at fifteen thousand feet, which was the height at which we intended to operate.

The ground from that height appears very unreal, rather like a beautifully painted large-scale map. Sometimes we left vapour trails behind us which looked like great spiral, horizontal columns of white smoke swirling in our wake: there were always four of them, one from each engine, and they completely obscured the aircraft formating behind us, as would a thick fog. Sometimes these great swirling, spiral trails followed us the whole time we were up at that height, and at other times they would cease for a few miles as suddenly as they had started, and then gush forth again. They were a nuisance when we were in formation, as they left the aeroplanes behind us enveloped in their swirling fog.

.   .   .   .   .

I chose Dick as our front gunner. I had never flown with him before, but I knew him to be sound. We had Freddy as our navigator, Joe as our wireless operator, Tom as our engineer, and Peter as second pilot. Robby seemed very pleased with his crew, and we were certainly happy with him.

The raid was detailed for December 18th, and the formation had reached a high standard of flying. On the night before the raid I had a bad bout of 'stage fright'. As I lay in bed my imagination got the better of me for a bit, and ran riot. All sorts of nightmarish horrors raced through my mind as I lay bathed in perspiration, despite the cold winter night. I saw fighters coming at us unmercifully from all directions . . . my turret was out of action, with me in it unable to fight back: I saw myself trapped in my turret with flames around me, and unable to conquer them: I heard and saw shells bursting about me, tearing through the aircraft and my turret: I saw myself having to land on the sea: all these and many other horrors were with me as I lay in the dark, trying to sleep. Very weak and foolish, no doubt, but there I was while I was at the mercy of my imagination. Nor was I free from imaginings when I was asleep, as that night I dreamt I was taken prisoner!

.   .   .   .   .

We were to take off at ten o'clock, and all the crews met in the crew-room before it was light to hear a final discussion of plans. We had been briefed the previous evening, so we knew what was expected of us.

The *Scharnhorst, Gneisnau,* and *Prince Eugen* were all lying in Brest harbour, and we were shown photographs and large-scale diagrams, as well as a coloured chalk drawing on the blackboard giving their exact positions. I knew most of these drawings by heart, having been to Brest before at night.

Brest is a very well-defended target, and of course during the time the ships were there the defences were very much increased. It was pretty evident that we should be in for a hot time. We were to have a strong fighter escort, which was a considerable comfort.

Altogether, there were forty bombers, consisting of sixteen Stirlings, fourteen Halifaxes, and ten Manchesters. The Stirlings were to lead the way in, followed by the Halifaxes, which in turn would be followed by the Manchesters.

There was a thick white frost when we went out to our aeroplanes, and it was still freezing hard. The ground crew were waiting for us, muffled in greatcoats, scarves, and Bala-clava helmets. Some of them were beating their arms across their chests, and stamping their feet, trying to get warm. Our aeroplane was gleaming white with frost, which glistened as the rays of the sun—just appearing above the horizon—glanced across it. The perspex round my turret was caked with an opaque white brine, which re-formed almost as soon as I wiped it away. I used a rag soaked in petrol, but even this froze almost at once, and it was obvious that I should have to wait for the frost to clear itself when we climbed to a drier atmosphere. Some airmen were standing on the wings and tail plane, sweeping away with brooms the frost, which fell to the ground like fine powdered snow.

The sun showing just above the hills in the distance was throwing its silver rays horizontally across the ground, and casting elongated and grotesque shadows from the aeroplanes. The ground shone and sparkled, crisp and clean: it was a per-fect English morning.

The Station Commander drove up with the A.O.C., who had come to see us off. They stopped and talked with us for a few minutes, and then wished us luck and moved off to the other aeroplanes.

It was time to start up, so we got in . . . and I pushed and struggled my way to my turret, where there was no room to spare. Shortly after we were airborne my perspex cleared itself of the frost and I was able to see out quite distinctly.

Wilkie was formating on our starboard, and Willie on our port. Wilkie was a tall, dark-haired, loose-limbed fellow, and the first impression a stranger might have of him could be that he was a rather irresponsible, carefree and vague in-dividual. But on closer acquaintance it would be seen that he had one of the kindest, gentlest, and most sympathetic and thoughtful natures any man could possess. Curiously enough, he was carrying the same gunner that Johnny had had on our previous daylight raid.

I have flown with Wilkie on two operational trips, so I know all his sterling qualities. He has the knack of inspiring con-fidence in every member of his crew. I certainly look back on the trips I did with him, which were to Brest and Wilhelms-haven, with very happy memories. When flying he is always perfectly calm, and I cannot imagine anything disturbing him.

Each time I reported back to him searchlights behind our tail, or flak bursts particularly near the tail, or fighters in the distance, he replied with one word—'Right'—spoken in a long-drawn-out way and in a manner to make you feel that all *was* right.

A good captain can inspire confidence and well-being in his crew by his manner, and by the way he speaks or replies. I have flown with some excellent captains, and I know! A good crew is like a happy family, all working together, thinking together and in an emergency acting together and for each other.

Willie was a young sergeant pilot, and one with whom I had always wanted to fly, but had never had the opportunity. He was a first-class pilot, but very modest, shy, and unobtrusive.

Robby, Wilkie, and Willie had been flying together in formation for the past nine days, and they knew each other's ways of flying perfectly.

Shortly after Wilkie and Willie formated on us, I saw our second formation of three come up and take their position about three hundred yards behind us. We climbed steadily, still circling the aerodrome, which appeared smaller and smaller and less distinct. In the distance I could see six more Halifaxes coming towards us, and as they came nearer I saw four more appear out of the blue. We still continued to climb and circle, while the others, in their turn, took up their positions in our rear.

When we reached ten thousand feet we set course in a south-westerly direction, and once again I watched and enjoyed the ever-changing panorama below us. The sun was slightly to my right, and almost enveloped Wilkie's aeroplane in its brilliance. I was well dressed to meet the cold, but all my clothes made movement in my turret well-nigh impossible. I sat with my hands on the control column, moving the turret every few minutes to prevent it freezing.

We crossed the Welsh mountains—looking rather like the relief maps you see in schools—and made our way towards Lundy Island, where we were to meet the Stirlings and Manchesters. The Stirlings had arrived there a few minutes before we did, and the Manchesters appeared as we formated behind the Stirlings.

So we set course for Brest . . . a long, formidable line of

determined might . . . on that cold, clear December morning.
There was very little cloud about, and I watched Lundy Island
—looking rather lonely—fade into the background of blue,
and then the rugged coast of Cornwall stretched away on
either side, fifteen thousand feet below. I was within a few
miles of my home, and I looked longingly down on this shore
that I know so well, and wondered what was happening there.

It did not take long to pass over this narrow stretch of
land, and we were soon over the sea again, well on the way
towards our objective. Our own land was gradually disappearing and getting farther away as the enemy got nearer.

As the French coast came in sight to those in front, I asked
Robby if he could see any fighters.

"Yes, plenty, but I can't see what they are yet."

'Well, we shall soon see,' I thought, and I hoped they were
our escort. There would be no difficulty in sighting our target,
as the sea stretched clear and blue below us, with only occasional wisps of fleecy cloud.

As was previously arranged, Wilkie dropped behind and
below us; Willie behind and below him; and the same with the
other three, as we neared the target. This was the formation
we intended to bomb from, and it would allow each of us to
bomb the target with a greater degree of accuracy. I looked
along the line bobbing up and down behind us, as I had seen
them so many times on our practice flights.

As we neared the target the guns opened on us. They had
been concentrating on the Stirlings, and now that we were
getting within range, they started on us! It was as I had
expected and experienced before, just as noisy, uncomfortable,
and unpleasant. The first few shells went above us, and to
starboard . . . but they soon corrected this, and we flew through
and into the puffs which a split second before had been
destructive, white hot, ragged chunks of steel.

As I looked down the line I saw the shells bursting around
each of the aeroplanes. Sometimes a shell seemed to burst right
on one of them, and I knew that only a split second and a
question of feet had saved it from complete destruction.
Once Willie was blown on to his side and almost on to his back,
and for a horrible moment I thought he was going down, as he
swung right out, shuddered on his side, and more shells burst
around him. However, he recovered in some miraculous

manner and resumed his place in the formation as though nothing had happened.

There were no fighters near us; our escort was seeing to that, but I could see them flying around in pairs some distance off. Once or twice I saw a scrap, but they were too far away for me to see much. I kept my turret moving continually, looking around me ready for the odd Jerry that might sneak through our screen.

I heard Robby say—"Bomb doors open!"—and knew that he would have sighted the target, and would be preparing for the bombing 'run-up'. Shells were bursting around us incessantly, causing our aeroplane to shudder and lurch. I saw the bomb doors open in the other aircraft down the line. We were all ready to drop our load.

The barrage seemed to be increasing in intensity, as though those below were determined we should never drop our bombs. They hoped to turn us back; make us waver or have us down, but I knew that nothing would make Robby take any evasive action until after he had dropped his bombs. We had not been practising for the past nine days and come all this way for nothing! The shells kept screaming and bursting around us as we went, six formidable monsters ready to pounce on our prey.

Freddy had got the ships in his sights, and was giving his 'lefts' and 'rights' and 'steady' . . . and, finally, *"Bombs gone!"* Each aircraft in turn released its bombs, and I saw them start their journey down. As they left their racks they seemed to hover for a second . . . and then drop rapidly, gradually pointing their noses to the ground.

While I watched the weight of bombs on their downward drop, Robby called to me:

"See if you can spot where they fall, Riv."

I leant forward, peering down, and as I watched I was hurled hard against the side of my turret while the aeroplane shuddered and rocked on its side, losing height rapidly. At the same time there was a crash like a breaking plate-glass window as shrapnel tore through my turret, ripping open the sleeve of my flying coat and tunic. I did not know if a piece had gone through me or not! I felt no pain, so imagined I had escaped.

The aeroplane was steady now, but was gradually losing height. Wilkie and Willie had taken up their positions again on either side, and kept close to us. Black smoke was belching past the tail from both port engines. I called through and told Robby, who said—"Yes, they're on fire." Would nothing upset the man? I wondered. The shells were still at us, mingling their smoke with the smoke from our engines.

"I think the fires are dying down," I heard Freddy say. The smoke was certainly less dense, and I began to think that there might be hope for us yet. That first sight of black dirty smoke rushing past my turret had seemed final, somehow. It does not take long for fire to spread in the air, and I knew the flames might gradually be getting nearer the wing tanks.

Yes, the smoke and sparks had ceased to gush out so fearfully, and had thinned down to a faint grey, which at last disappeared altogether. Both engines had stopped, and we were listing hard to starboard. The port wing had taken the brunt of the shock as the shell burst: it must have burst just in front of the wing, hurtling splinters through both engines.

The shells had ceased, and Brest was disappearing behind us. Wilkie and Willie were still with us, like faithful dogs following their weary master home.

"Send out an S O S. We're coming down in the sea!"

Time seemed to stand still as I heard Robby say this to Joe. It was as though a death sentence had been passed on me. So my nightmare of the previous night was coming true, after all! I felt empty inside. God! I had done this before. . . . I knew what it was like.

"Can't you make it, sir?" I called through to Robby.

"No. I'm afraid you're in for another ducking, Riv, old boy."

"How much longer, sir?"

"Ten more minutes."

Ten more minutes! What then? Was this to be the end, after all? I knew no Halifax had as yet landed on the sea and got away with it. How should we fare? As we hit the water, would it be the end? . . . or would we float for days, getting weaker all the time?

What would happen? Ten more minutes . . . less now. *Oh, hell! This won't do!* We were still alive, and there might be hope. Yes, there was always a chance! We were still alive . . . and we were clear of Brest! That was what really mattered.

Five more minutes now! There was silence down the

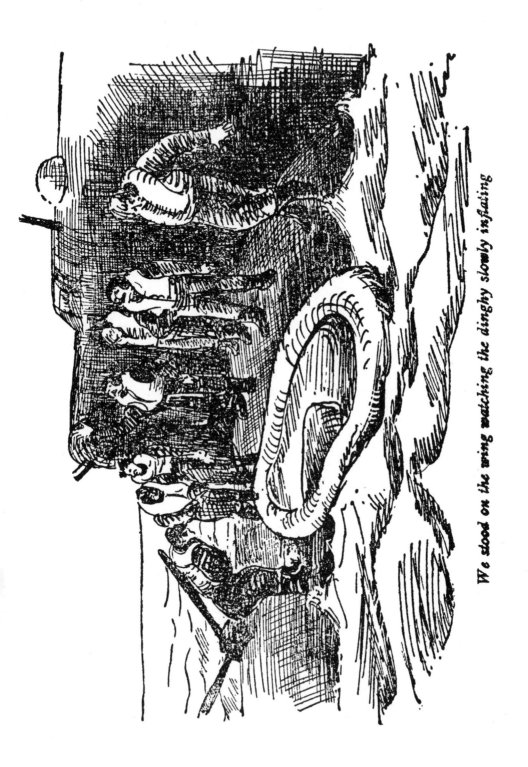

We stood on the wing watching the dinghy slowly inflating

intercom., except for Joe's tapping on the morse key as he methodically sent out S O S's.

"Stand by for ditching!"

I hurriedly left my turret and went forward. My actions were mechanical. I knew what to do: 'Mae West' inflated, boots tightly strapped, flying clothing fastened, helmet on and also securely fastened, these things I looked to as I made my way forward, pushing and squeezing my way past the tail wheel leg, through the rear bulkhead door, and so to the centre of the fuselage.

As I passed by the side fuselage windows I looked down at the sea, so calm and blue, yet as hard as concrete to hit. I opened the rear escape hatch in the roof, ready for a hasty exit.

Freddy and Dick were already in the fuselage, and they were followed by Joe, Sam, and Peter. All exchanged what were intended to be reassuring smiles. Freddy and I lay on the floor with our feet braced against the main spar, and the others were farther forward on the beds. So we waited . . . for what?

As I lay looking up at the blue sky through the open hatch above my head, my thoughts raced, tumbling over each other. What would happen? I knew all the hazards of a sea landing, chancy at the best of times, but with two engines on the same side gone, more than doubly so. I heard the engines throttle back, and prepared myself for the shock . . . body braced, muscles tense. We glided silently for a few seconds, seconds that seemed like minutes. There was a deafening crash; a rush of icy water as we were hurled forward, and then, oh, joy! we were *floating*!

Ten minutes which seemed like a lifetime were over. I climbed out of the rear escape hatch at the same time as Robby came out of the forward one. As he poked his head out he greeted me with an enormous belch which seemed to relieve his feelings somewhat.

"Nice work, sir," I said, referring to his ditching, not his belch.

"Well . . . we made it O.K. Everyone all right?" he asked.

By this time we were all standing clustered on the wing, watching the dinghy slowly opening. Oh, glorious sight! . . . the yellow dinghy unfolding and inflating in the sunshine ready to receive us.

Wilkie and Willie were circling round us, and we were

waving up at them and laughing . . . yes, laughing. We were gay and happy, and had every cause to be. The odds had been more against than for us. By now we might have been dead, crushed and mangled by the broken, twisted aeroplane: or struggling in the darkness with our lungs full of water as the aeroplane sank below the surface to the botton, never to be seen again.

The dinghy was ready for us—big and round and secure: it was more than twice the size of the last one I had been in. We pushed it off the wing and stepped gingerly in, all excepting Robby, who still stood on the wing waving his arms wildly to the circling aircraft.

"Anyone want anything from inside?" he asked. "I'm going to have a look at her."

He climbed on to the top of the fuselage, took a deep breath, and lowered himself inside. I wished he would stop fooling about and come and join us: I was scared stiff that the aeroplane would sink with him inside it.

After a bit he reappeared and sat on the hatch with his legs dangling inside. "She's filling up," he said.

"What about getting in the dinghy, sir?" I asked.

"No hurry yet, Riv. I'm going back in a moment to try and find my pipe."

Well, you can't very well call your C.O. a B.F., even if you think he is one!

He took another deep breath and disappeared once more. The aeroplane was more than half full of water, and I thought in danger of sinking at any moment.

After what seemed an uncomfortably long time, Robby appeared—without his pipe—and at last joined us. As he got in there was a nasty hissing sound just behind me, and I looked round to see a jagged hole from which the air was rapidly escaping. There were some large wooden stoppers handy for just such an emergency, and I hurriedly screwed one in. The dinghy had rubbed hard against a damaged bit of the wing, which had caused the trouble. We shoved her off from the wing, and floated some yards away from the aircraft.

"Well, Riv, what do we do now?" Robby asked. "You ought to know . . . as you've done this sort of thing before."

"We don't do anything. We just sit!"

"Has anyone got a pack of cards?"

"There might be one in here," Freddy said. He was undoing a large canvas satchel.

It did not contain any cards, however, but was full of tinned food, distress signals, first-aid kit, cigarettes and matches. The cigarettes were passed round, and we lit up.

"Anyone hungry? . . . or shall we wait?" Robby asked.

We decided to wait, in case we should really need the food later. We had a drink of water each, though, as we were feeling a little dry after swallowing so much of the salt sea.

Wilkie was still circling us. He had climbed up to a few thousand feet, and was obviously wirelessing our position and calling for help. It was a comforting sight, seeing him there, and knowing that we were not alone or forgotten. Already the vast air-sea rescue service would be busy sending out search planes, and informing any ships in our vicinity.

Willie had disappeared, and had presumably returned to base. We watched Wilkie for some time in silence.

I was profoundly thankful, and curiously at peace and happy, thinking how different this was to the last time I had been floating in a dinghy. The sea was quite calm, with only a slight swell which caused us to rise up and down with a regular rhythmical movement, rather like a swing after it has died down and is just swaying to and fro.

"My arse is wet," Robby said, after a long silence. "Let's see if we can get the inside of this dinghy dry."

We were sitting round the edge with our feet in the middle, and the water kept lapping over the side, washing against our bottoms, which was distinctly uncomfortable. There were several inches of water in the bottom of the dinghy. We tried scooping it up, but had nothing effective with which to do it. . . so soaked it up with our gloves and scarves, which were wet anyway. By working fairly hard this way we were able to keep the inside reasonably dry.

Wilkie had evidently done all he could, for he came down and skimmed a few feet over the sea right by us, and flew off out of sight. I felt rather lonely after he had gone, and missed the sound of his engines. While he was flying around us we seemed to have some definite contact with our own country, and I felt that at any rate someone knew where we were. He had stayed with us for half an hour, and I wondered how long it would be before we saw someone else besides ourselves.

We were alone, except for our Halifax floating a few yards away from us. She was a pathetic sight, lying there so helpless and impotent . . . gradually getting lower in the water and looking as though she might go down at any moment. Her wings were awash, with the wake lapping against the sides of the fuselage.

I looked at my turret, with the guns showing just above the water. It seemed strange to think that not so long before I had been sitting in that turret looking down on the sea on which we were now floating.

The nose of the aeroplane dropped lower in the sea: she rolled slowly over on her side, raising her scarred port wing majestically to the sky . . . and gradually disappeared, leaving only a swirl of water to mark her grave. We were silent for some time, and I think all of us felt rather sad. We were alone now, surrounded by the vast expanse of the slowly moving sea.

"Does anyone know a song?" Robby asked, after a bit . . . and, without waiting for a reply, he started on the tune of the 'Volga Boatmen'.

On the whole, we were a very cheerful party. Our chances of being picked up were fairly good, as it was definitely known that we were on the sea, and our position fixed. Only some extraordinarily bad luck—such as the dinghy sinking, some sudden storm or fog—could prevent us from being saved. I don't think the thought of being picked up by an enemy ship occurred to us, although we were considerably nearer to the French coast than to our own. Once or twice as I looked at the rolling mass of blue about us my heart seemed to miss a beat as I foresaw several days of floating, unseen by any searchers; but these pangs were only momentary, and for the most part I felt reasonably cheerful.

I sat with Robby on one side of me and Joe on the other. Freddy was opposite me with Dick, and Sam and Peter on either side of him.

"How are you feeling, Freddy?" I asked. "You're looking a bit green!"

"I'm *feeling* a bit green," he replied and, suiting his actions to his words, was sick over the side.

This apparently was too much for Dick, as he did likewise. This created some slight diversion for us, as we offered sundry advice all round!

"I could do with a drink!" Robby said.

"I've got a flask of rum."

"Come on, Riv, *out with it*! Let's have a swig."

"No! Let's wait until we see some help, and then celebrate."

"Good idea."

So we sat, sometimes talking, sometimes silent; for the most part cheerful, and all the time looking around and listening for the help that should come. We began reckoning how long it would take for a rescue boat to arrive, and what sort of a boat or ship they would send for us.

Robby said to me—"Could you see the bombs burst, Riv?"

"No, sir. There was so much smoke around the ships that I couldn't be certain. It looked to me as though they were on fire."

"I got a *wizard* sight," Freddy declared. "I swear the bombs dropped right across the ships. They must have been hit!"

"Good show."

"What time does it get dark?" Sam asked after a bit.

"About five o'clock. Why?"

"I was just wondering how much longer we'd got before dark, that was all."

"Oh, we've got another hour or two yet."

"*I can hear an aeroplane!*" Peter suddenly said. "Yes, there it is. Look!"

"It's a Lysander," someone announced.

"Where's that *flask*, Riv?"

"Hold on, sir. Let's make certain first."

The Lysander was approaching, flying on a zig-zag course about five hundred feet up, and making more or less in our direction.

"Get the pistol ready, Freddy!" Robby said.

"Don't fire it too soon," I suggested. "Wait until it comes a bit closer."

It was getting steadily nearer, and we all watched it anxiously. When it was about half a mile away, Freddy fired the 'Verey' pistol. The signal must have been seen, for the Lysander immediately turned in our direction, and flew over us, flashing an answering light.

I passed my flask to Robby, and we drank to the Lysander circling above us. One stage towards our rescue was over, and I hoped the next would be as easy.

The Lysander flew round and round us for about an hour, and then, without any warning, turned off out of sight. . . .

Oh, hell! What's happening now? Surely it can't be getting low in petrol, and leaving us?

We waited anxiously, watching the spot where it had disappeared, and in a few minutes we saw it reappear again and come towards us. It circled us once more; fired a 'Verey' cartridge, and then went off again in the same direction as before . . . only to reappear again, firing another cartridge. It repeated that performance several times, and the reason was obvious: it had seen a ship and was guiding it towards us.

Presently three dots appeared on the horizon, and gradually took the shape of boats. Our joy and relief were terrific, and we waved to the Lysander and shouted and sang until the ships drew alongside. There was a motor launch escorted by two motor torpedo-boats.

The motor launch threw us a line and hauled us alongside.

"Hop in, Riv," Robby said.

"*Hop's* about the right word, sir. I think I've broken my foot. . . ."

"You bloody fool! Why the hell didn't you say so before?"

"Well, there wasn't much point, was there?"

·   ·   ·   ·   ·

We were hauled aboard, and once more I took off wet clothes in front of a roaring stove.

Rum and cigarettes were pressed on us, and we felt very much at home and content. The skipper was a marvellous host, and he waited on us and fussed round us continuously.

Robby was lamenting the fate of his favourite pipe, now at the bottom of the sea, and the skipper said:

"My dear chap! I've the very thing for you. It hasn't been smoked . . . and I don't like it, anyway. It's *yours*!"

Robby took it gratefully, and lit up.

·   ·   ·   ·   ·

"What about the news?" the skipper said at six o'clock.

"A strong force of our bombers attacked Brest in daylight today . . ." we heard.

·   ·   ·   ·   ·

Looking back, I remember an evening of smoking, dozing, talking, and drinking rum. It was an evening of content and complete happiness, and one I shall always remember. The skipper and his crew talked to us, asking innumerable questions. We fixed up future meetings . . . and the whole evening went far too quickly!

.   .   .   .   .

We were taken off to hospital when we got ashore, much to Robby's disgust. He wanted a party, and protested at some length . . . but without the desired result.

We arrived back at our unit late the following night, and were met by half the squadron, who turned up at the railway station to welcome us. I was supported between Freddy and Joe.

.   .   .   .   .

A few days after Christmas the squadron was detailed **to go** again to Brest.

Robby had a new gunner in my place. I was merely **a** spectator, and I felt rather out of it.

As I stood, leaning on my crutches, watching the **crews** pile into the transport to take them to their aeroplanes, Robby said to me—"I wish you were coming with us, Riv!"

"So do I, sir."

THE END